A PARTISAN'S MEMOIR

WOMAN OF THE HOLOCAUST

by

Faye Schulman

With the assistance of
SARAH SILBERSTEIN SWARTZ

SECOND STORY *Press*

Canadian Cataloguing in Publication Data

Schulman, Faye
A partisan's memoir : woman of the Holocaust

ISBN 0 929005 76-7

1. Schulman, Faye. 2. Holocaust, Jewish (1939-1945) –
Poland – Lenin – Personal narratives. 3. World War, 1939-1945 –
Underground movements – Poland – Lenin – Biography.
4. Jews – Poland – Lenin – Biography. I. Title.

DS135.P63S35 1995   940.53'18'092   C95-932478-X

With the assistance of Sarah Silberstein Swartz
Edited by Rhea Tregebov

Cover design: Liz Martin
Production assistance: Michael Kelly

Printed and bound in Canada

*Second Story Press gratefully acknowledges the assistance
of The Canada Council and the Ontario Arts Council*

Second Story Press
720 Bathurst Street Suite 301
Toronto, ON
M5S 2R4

Let this book be a monument ...

*To the memory of my beloved family, my father, my mother,
two sisters and two brothers, who perished at the
hands of the Nazi murderers;*

*To the partisans who died fighting for
Jewish dignity, honour and peace;*

*To the future of our Jewish youth — including my
grandchildren Michael, Daniel, Nathan, Matthew,
Rachelle and Steven — who continue the Jewish heritage
and carry on the memory.*

CONTENTS

PREFACE

I HAVE BEEN WRITING this book in my mind for half a century. The memories are still vivid and it is now time to put them on paper, to record this crucial part of history as reflected in my own experiences.

As a member of the Holocaust Education and Memorial Centre and the Yad Vashem Committee in Toronto I have spoken of my experiences as a partisan and a survivor of the Holocaust at public schools and universities, at teachers' seminars, convents and ecumenical gatherings. The photographs of atrocity I was forced to process for the Nazis and those I took myself during the war have become part of this telling. My audiences have been Jewish and gentile, young students and older people, clergy and teachers. Those most affected by my testimony have been young people with little or no previous knowledge of the Holocaust. One girl who attended my workshop with other students from a Catholic school wrote: "My ideas have changed. I feel such shame that anti-Jewish feelings would be the basis of such a horror story. Our danger for the future lies in forgetting such a black past. Forgetting the Holocaust would be to blind ourselves to the darker side of humanity."

With the publication of my story in book form, I hope the audience for this account will expand beyond my geographical boundaries and beyond my lifetime. It is my hope that those who read *A Partisan's Memoir* will gain from it a greater understanding of the difficult life, struggle and heroism of Jewish partisans in the resistance during the Holocaust.

Too many have denied the Holocaust. Even more have perpetuated the myth of passivity, the fallacy that six million Jews went docilely to their deaths, like lambs to the slaughter. It is important that future generations should know this to be untrue. In reality, wherever there was the slightest opportunity, Jews fought back. The Jewish people did their utmost to survive under unfathomably difficult circumstances in the forests, in the ghettos, and in the camps. We all fought for our lives and for the lives of our loved ones. Many fought with weapons in hand in the ghettos, as underground fighters in occupied cities and villages, as partisans in the forest, and simply as individuals who resisted those who came to destroy them.

Inevitably, the majority of those unsung heroes and heroines who fought as partisans did not survive. Yet their bravery and courageous qualities should never be forgotten. We shall never know the precise number of the anonymous dead. As one of the survivors, I feel compelled to speak for those who were tragically silenced. So little has been written — it has almost been kept a secret — about the bravery of the Jewish partisans. I served in the partisan resistance, as one of thousands of Jewish men and women who joined the partisan movement and engaged in daily attacks, ambushes and battles against the enemy. We faced hunger and cold; we faced the constant threat of death and torture; added to this we faced anti-Semitism in our own ranks. Against all odds, we struggled against Nazi oppression. We used every available resource, all our courage, spirit and inventiveness, to combat the enemy. Many partisan fighters were mere children — teenagers like myself — entrusted with the weight of adult responsibility. They never gave up. They fought for revenge, for honour and dignity, for an end to the murder and an end to the war, many to their last breath.

It is important to keep in mind that my story is only one of a multitude of stories of Jewish survivors. Although each story is unique, each is also representative; all are invaluable. The documentation of these first-person testimonies is crucial; it is through them that we can forcefully and successfully challenge the myths and present the truth.

ACKNOWLEDGEMENTS

I would like to thank my daughter Susan, my son Sidney and my daughter-in-law Louise for giving me the emotional support, the confidence and the inspiration to complete the writing of this book.

I will be eternally grateful to my husband Morris, blessed be his memory, for sharing my life and encouraging me to document the most difficult years of my life. Sadly, he is no longer with me to see my task accomplished.

I would also like to acknowledge the efforts of Maureen Mazin, David Birkan and Lisa Ben Simon whose help and encouragement was appreciated.

Special gratitude and appreciation to Sarah Swartz for her invaluable work and for her deep understanding.

INTRODUCTION

*I*T WAS TOWARDS the end of the year 1942. Our detachment of partisan fighters had been given an order to leave our base in the woods for another raid on the town of Lenin. Misha, the Russian leader of our brigade, had sent us on a mission to strike at the enemy. This time we were to raze the houses used as headquarters by the Nazis and their collaborators. After the initial gunfire, there would be the usual brief lull before the arrival of Nazi reinforcements during which we would be able to seize any necessary supplies for survival in the forest: rifles, ammunition, food and medical supplies.

I had personal reasons for wanting to join in the assault of the town of Lenin. This was the *shtetl* which I had called home. Here I had been born and had lived with my family in the house lovingly built by my father. Here I had been raised with my six siblings and had experienced my youth. It was also the town where members of my own family had been murdered by the Nazis.

The *shtetl* of Lenin in the district of eastern Poland called Polesie, near the border to the Soviet Union, had held a community of six thousand Jews. On August 14, 1942 the entire remaining Jewish population of Lenin, except for myself and five other families, had been shot and buried in a few hours in three mass graves. Only myself and a few others escaped death. After three years of war, I found myself, at the age of nineteen, without a family, a home or a community.

Lenin was situated in a deserted region surrounded by swamps, rivers and dense forest good for camouflage. This was an ideal shelter for partisan bases such as ours. After the annihilation of our entire Jewish community, I had fled into the woods and joined the Molotava Brigade, a partisan detachment made up mostly of Russian soldiers and officers who had escaped from Nazi prison camps. I had been with the Molotava Brigade for six weeks and had participated in previous attacks. Now some of my colleagues informed me that preparations were under way for another attack on my home town of Lenin. I wanted to join the group in their attack on the murderers of my community, my own family. Initially, the commander had not intended to include me on this particular mission, but I begged for permission to go. I explained how important it was for me to continue to avenge the deaths of my loved ones by participating in such attacks. After some deliberation, he allowed me to join in the raid.

Our scouts had given us all the latest details of the town's activities. We knew exactly which houses the Nazis now occupied and how many Nazis and collaborators were in each house. We knew which buildings housed Gestapo headquarters, the *Wehrmacht*, and the local police who served the Nazi government. We also had a list of names and addresses of local civilians who had sympathized with the Nazis and abused their power over the rest of the population.

Our scouts had also learned from the peasants in the vicinity that the Nazis were experiencing difficulties keeping covered the three trenches where over 1,850 Jewish men, women and children had been murdered and buried. The Nazis had covered the graves with dirt and sand, but days later the grounds still continued to shift as the bodies settled; the top layer cracked and blood continued to seep out. Three times they covered the graves; three times the graves opened, like a giant bleeding wound. When I heard this news, it became impossible for me to remain behind while my own family's blood still flowed from the trenches. How could I not take part in our attack on Lenin?

It was not yet dawn when our band of ninety partisans reached the outskirts of Lenin. We had walked for hours during the night through the woods, avoiding the roads. Each had to be careful not to lose sight of the person immediately ahead, or risk becoming lost in the darkness. Now that we were outside the town, we separated into smaller groups and moved in closer to our assigned positions. At a given signal, we were to attack from all directions. If a Nazi guard noticed us before we received our signal, we had been instructed to strangle him to prevent his sounding the alarm.

⚶

I wait in silence amongst the pine trees on the outskirts of the town. The town is achingly familiar to me; every street, every corner brings back memories. I hold a loaded rifle firmly in my hands. Not far from where I am standing are the three trenches where members of my family and my friends were so brutally murdered. Overwhelmed by emotion, I imagine again this picture of horror. If I could, I would lie down on the ground, stretch out my arms and embrace the blood-soaked earth. I want to close my eyes and fall asleep with my loved ones forever. Instead I see their faces, I hear their voices whispering, "No! Don't give up. Now you have a rifle. Fight! Avenge us and defend yourself." I am no longer afraid. I hold my loaded rifle firmly in my hands.

This reverie is interrupted by a single shot fired into the stillness: our signal to advance. From our various entrenchments around the buildings, all ninety of us shriek a loud

"Hurrah! Hurrah!" to unnerve the Nazis as we begin shooting. We burn their headquarters down over their heads.

I am shooting blindly ahead. I do not see the faces into which I fire. Some of the startled Nazi guards stationed outside the buildings retaliate with their own gunfire. Dead and wounded on both sides. An eerie quiet descends.

I find myself near my family's house and run inside. I am choked with emotion. This house had always been full of life, of people coming and going — relatives, friends, neighbours. And now total silence. The rooms empty, the home's rightful occupants dead. Potato peelings litter the floor where the Nazis had dropped them. Hearing our gunshots, they had departed in terror only moments ago. From our partisan informers, I know that my former home has sheltered about thirty local collaborators who work as Nazi policemen.

I stand in the centre of the room, transfixed, dry-eyed. In my mind I hear a strange urgent cry. It is my mother's voice. A cry with an echo. I see images of my sisters, my brother. Yes, I hear them all crying — a cry of the innocent, demanding remembrance: "Run! Fight! Resist!" That cry gives me no peace. I clench my fists. I myself cannot cry. No time for tears. The tension, the necessities of the moment overrule my inner feelings.

Another partisan runs into the house. It is Moishe, whom we have nicknamed *der Weisser*, the blond. "This is your house. What do you think?" he bellows. "Shall we burn it down?"

My family is dead; my town has been occupied. I will never live here again. I do not want the murderers to have the use of our home. In less time than it takes to form these thoughts, I shout back at him, "Burn it!" He pours gasoline on the living room floor. I light the matches. The house is instantly ablaze. As we retreat to the safety of the forest, I

The ruins of the Lazebnik family home; only the chimneys stand.

turn my head to watch the flames and smoke breaking through the sky. I feel heartbroken, devastated — something precious has been lost yet again. Still more ties to my past are irrevocably severed. A terrible truth: this town and this house, so close to my heart, are no more. I can still hear the screams coming from the three trenches; they are forever engraved in my mind.

POLAND 1930

LATVIA

BALTIC SEA

LITHUANIA

GERMANY

EAST PRUSSIA

Vilna

Minsk

Vistula River

Bialystok

BELORUSSIAN SSR

Brest-Litovsk

Pinsk

Warsaw

Pripet River

Lodz

Lublin

Bug River

Cracow

Lvov

Tarnopol

UKRAINIAN SSR

CZECHOSLOVAKIA

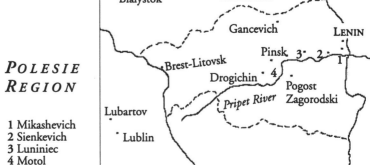

POLESIE REGION

1 Mikashevich
2 Sienkevich
3 Luniniec
4 Motol

Bialystok

Baranovich

Gancevich

LENIN

Pinsk   3   2

1

Brest-Litovsk

Drogichin   4

Pogost Zagorodski

Lubartov

Pripet River

Lublin

CHRONOLOGY

September 1, 1939: Poland is invaded by the Nazis and the Soviet Union. Poland is divided between Nazi Germany to the west and the Soviet Union to the east. The town of Lenin comes under Soviet occupation.

June 22, 1941: The Nazis attack Soviet-occupied Poland and the Soviet Union without warning, despite the two countries' mutual non-aggression pact.

June 24, 1941: Nazi troops invade the Polish town of Lenin; the reign of terror begins.

May 1942: Transports begin of able-bodied Jewish men and boys from Lenin to the forced labour camps at Gancevich and elsewhere.

May 10, 1942: The Nazis create a Jewish ghetto in Lenin.

August 14, 1942: The Jewish ghetto in Lenin is eradicated; over 1,850 Jews are murdered, shot and buried in three mass graves. Only Faye Lazebnik and five other Jewish families survive. The Jews in the forced labour camp in Gancevich hear of the murders and decide to flee the camp. Many are killed in the escape, but most find refuge in the woods.

September 1942: Partisans from the Molotava Brigade raid Lenin; Faye Lazebnik escapes to join them. For the next two years, she will act as nurse and photographer to her partisan unit, as well as participate in many raids against the Nazi forces.

November 1942: Faye is briefly reunited with her brother Kopel, who has managed to escape Gancevich and join a partisan group. Faye rescues and assumes responsibility for an eight year old Jewish orphan, Raika Kliger.

December 1942: Lenin is razed by the Nazis, its remaining White Russian population burned to death.

February 1944: Faye's charge, Raika Kliger, is evacuated with the wounded to safety in Moscow.

February to March 1944: Nazi troops and collaborators force the Molotava Brigade to scatter from their base camp. Faye's unit, relentlessly pursued by the Nazis, miraculously survives and returns six weeks later to base.

July 3, 1944: Soviet troops liberate partisan territory of the Molotava Brigade; the Nazis are finally driven out. The partisans of the Molotava Brigade liberate the city of Pinsk.

December 12, 1944: Faye marries Morris Schulman.

June 1948: Faye, Morris and their daughter Susan emigrate to Canada.

Chapter One

LIFE IN OUR TOWN OF LENIN

*L*ENIN WAS NOT named after the communist revolutionary by that name; the town predated the Russian Revolution of 1917 by many years. Close to two hundred years ago, the town and its surrounding farms and villages had been owned by a wealthy aristocrat who had one daughter named Lena. He had named this town after her.

Lenin, the Polish town of my birth, stood on the shore of the Sluch River. On the other side of the river was the Soviet Union. A scrupulously guarded bridge, the only bridge for many kilometres, separated the two countries. Even before the beginning of the Second World War, the townspeople had been forbidden to approach the river, which served as a border. Only a few times in the year, when the sweltering summer days became almost unbearable, did the Polish military government grant us permission to swim in a small fenced-off section along the shoreline.

At the time of my childhood, Lenin had a civilian population of about 12,000. About half the inhabitants were Jewish. In addition, thousands of Polish soldiers and cavalrymen and their families were stationed in our town because of its strategic location. Their impressive headquarters and army barracks overshadowed most of the modest buildings in town. Only our large, modern hospital, located in a beautiful pine grove just at the outskirts of town, could compete in prestige.

Because Lenin was a border town, it was well guarded by the Polish armed forces. Even during the relatively quiet Polish rule, there were regulations and restrictions which had to be followed by all civilians of Lenin. A curfew was set at eleven at night and was strictly adhered to. Those who violated this curfew — such as young lovers meeting for a late night rendezvous — risked being caught and arrested. All visitors had to obtain a special permit to enter Lenin. This meant that visiting friends and relatives from other towns could not drop by without the formality of a visa. It also curtailed commerce between people from Lenin and those outside the vicinity, since making contact for business outside of Lenin was often complicated.

Without easy access to the outside world, the townspeople felt a kinship towards each other. Jews and gentiles lived in harmony with their neighbours. Although anti-Semitism was prevalent in other parts of Poland and in the Soviet Union, in Lenin there was an acceptance and understanding between Jew and Christian, at least on a personal level. I remember the whole town, Christians and Jews alike, celebrating the priest's fiftieth anniversary of service to the church in our town. The Jewish community honoured him by presenting him with a book bound in gold covers.

Though before the Second World War the town was part of Poland, the majority of the non-Jewish permanent inhabitants were White Russians, or Belorussians, as they were called. Still, Lenin was a Polish town and all official business was conducted in Polish. Until the age of fourteen, all the children of the town attended Polish public schools where the language of instruction was Polish. Every Jewish child had to

Lenin before the war; mid-1930s. Under the Nazis,
this area became the ghetto.

learn four languages: White Russian in the street, Polish in public school, Yiddish in the home, and Hebrew in *cheder*, the afternoon Jewish school that we all attended.

Though anti-Semitism was generally non-existent amongst the majority White Russian population in Lenin, attitudes towards Jews within the Polish minority varied. Two stories typify the extremes displayed by the town's Polish minority towards Jews. One day a neighbour, a shopkeeper named Olshevski who considered himself part of the Polish "elite" of our town, strolled by our house. My mother sat on our porch resting after a long day of hard work. The shopkeeper stopped to chat with my mother. After the usual formalities of normal conversation, he suddenly blurted out, "Mrs. Lazebnik, there will soon come a time when I will have the right to shoot all the Jewish people in this town."

My mother shot back, "Mr. Olshevski, there will soon come a time when a big hole will appear in front of you and you will fall in and never be able to get out again."

Later, when the Nazis occupied our town, Olshevski demanded that Jews come to clean his house. I became one of his scrub girls. If I didn't comply, he threatened to lodge a complaint with the Nazis. Some time after this, on one of their raids, the partisans shot Olshevski and others like him.

At the other extreme, a Polish captain, a physician, was a good friend to our family. During his daily walk every morning, he dropped by our house for a bottle of beer which my mother sold from our house to augment our family's livelihood. One day he noticed that my mother had been crying. When he asked her why, she told him she had no money to pay for my sister Sonia's upcoming wedding. While my mother went into the cellar to get the beer, the officer wrote out a cheque for five hundred zlotys. He handed it to her as payment for his beer and said, "I hope this will be sufficient."

Five hundred zlotys in those days was a fortune: enough for everything — the wedding, clothes, food and the rent for an apartment. This Polish officer made it possible for my sister to get married. My mother said that a good angel had come to visit her.

Despite government regulations and restrictions, before the Second World War the Jews of Lenin did manage to make a living. Jewish craftspeople, tradespeople and storekeepers made their income catering to the Polish officers and their families. The officers regularly organized special events for themselves — dances, parties and horse races. They even had their own orchestra with over two hundred musicians. And for all these occasions, their wives were always beautifully dressed, requiring the services of the talented Jewish seamstresses and tailors of the town.

*Lenin before the war; mid-1930s. Every spring
the lake flooded the streets of the town.*

Lenin had many acres of orchard land; it was one of the
largest fruit-growing districts in all of Poland. In the late summer, these groves of fruit trees were laden with ripe apples and
pears. Jewish merchants were often the middlemen in selling
and shipping these fruits and other produce across Poland.

There were two synagogues in town and only one church.
On Sundays, Christian villagers and farmers came from the
outskirts of town to attend church, and at the same time
brought with them a variety of produce to exchange with
Jewish shopkeepers for shoes, clothing, soap and a special delicacy — fresh white rolls baked by the Jewish bakers in
Lenin. These rolls were very different from the coarse dark
whole-wheat breads eaten every day. After church services,
people gathered in the hundreds to chat, to barter and to eat
their lunches of fresh white rolls just purchased from the
Jewish merchants.

Lenin's Jewish community was a vibrant one. The community had its own cemetery and burial society to take care

of its deceased, its own *bet din*, a "court" held for internal disputes among Jews, its own benevolent society to help the Jewish poor. After their public school day, Jewish children attended *cheder*, a supplementary school maintained by the community. At *cheder* they were taught to read Hebrew, the Torah and other religious books.

Most of the Jews in town were observant Jews who practised Judaism with great devotion. They were known as *misnagdim*. Because they wore contemporary European dress and were clean-shaven, they were considered more modern than their chasidic counterparts in other areas of the country. The chasidim wore long beards, sidelocks and the traditional long black coats and fur hats that had characterized Jews from earlier times. Yet the Jews in our community were also religious Orthodox. They prayed three times a day, kept kosher households, and adhered to the Jewish customs, rituals and laws that had been passed down to them for generations.

In Lenin, Jewish holidays were openly celebrated with great enthusiasm by the entire Jewish community. As a child, I recall joining my *cheder* schoolmates on a hike in the woods to celebrate Lag B'omer, the springtime holiday commemorating Bar Kochba's revolt against the Romans. We romped through the trees with our bows and arrows, as was customary for this holiday, singing and dancing in celebration. We brought with us a huge picnic with abundant food and drink for everyone to share.

On the Sabbath and each Jewish holiday, the streets were filled with young people promenading in groups arm-in-arm, singing at the tops of our voices the Hebrew and Yiddish songs we had learned at home and in *cheder*. Never was there any fear of persecution or trouble from the gentile population.

I especially remember the street celebrations on Simchas Torah, the holiday which celebrates the completion of the annual cycle of the reading of the Torah, the Five Books of Moses, and the beginning of the first reading. The entire community took part in a procession, carrying the rabbi from his home to the synagogue. Men, women and children danced through the streets of the town, singing with great zeal as they held up the Torah scrolls and kissed them in communal rejoicing.

It became a custom in our town during this celebration for neighbours to sneak into each others' homes and steal a huge pot of food from the kitchen to bring to the synagogue for everyone to share a meal after the services. Women would cook huge vats of *tsimmes*, a traditional holiday dish made with carrots, potatoes and prunes, and leave it in their unlocked homes — just in case.

Family celebrations and life cycle events such as births, bar mitzvahs, weddings and funerals were communally celebrated. A wedding party might include hundreds of guests, since the whole community was usually invited. Everyone was served sweet wine, sponge cake and honey cake, symbols of a sweet future life.

People in our town were very interested in politics and in what was going on in the rest of the world, especially in Palestine and Poland. They subscribed to newspapers in many languages from all over Europe. Often Jewish speakers from other parts of Poland were invited to address the community — provided they could get the documents to allow entry in this closely guarded border town.

Though some Jews in Lenin were involved with socialist organizations, their numbers were limited. Because of our proximity to the Soviet Union — considered "the enemy" by the Polish government — and the strict Polish surveillance put on us, it was dangerous to be known as an active member of the Communist Party. For example, on the first of May, an important communist holiday, we were always careful not to wear the colour red as red was the symbol of communism. Wearing red might be construed as a sign of support for the Soviet Union; we were afraid it could result in our arrest by the local Polish regiment.

Adults and teenagers participated in various other social and political activities. In the library, young members organized their own book reviews, presentations and lectures. This became a special social haven for Jewish youth. Here young people would meet to share intellectual and political ideas as well as to socialize.

Many young people became active members in various Zionist movements, varying from the religious *Betar* and *Mizrachi* movements to the left wing *Chalutz* and *Shomer Hazair*. Though the ideologies of these organizations differed, they all aspired to the establishment of an independent Jewish state in Palestine. Young and old donated their time to *Keren Kayemet*, the organization which raised funds for the establishment of a Jewish state.

Many women belonged to a Jewish volunteer sisterhood which collected food and clothing from the rich and gave it to the poor. I recall my mother going to the homes of the affluent families in town every Friday afternoon, basket in hand, to collect *challahs*, special egg loaves for the Sabbath meal, for the poor who could not afford to bake them. The sisterhood also organized care for the community's sick, the old, the hungry. In winter they distributed warm clothing and shoes to children who otherwise went without. Younger women met regularly to knit and embroider tablecloths and linens which they later raffled off to raise money for charity.

For entertainment, we had our own local theatre group which staged Yiddish classics like *Tevye the Milkman*, *Mirele Efros* and *The Dybuk*. Though the actors and musicians were amateurs, the quality of their performances were first rate and they took their work in the theatre very seriously. Plays and musical performances were held in a building with a grand stage which was rented especially for these performances by the Jewish community from the Polish military. The money from the sale of tickets went for expenses and any leftover funds were sent to the poor or to *Keren Kayemet* for Palestine.

Conversation was another form of recreation in this isolated town. After a theatre performance people talked, after a wedding they talked, and after funerals they also talked. Stories and jokes were constantly told and retold until the original of the tale was hardly recognizable.

I remember a story about an elderly couple which was constantly repeated. One day the wife got sick. She went to the doctor, who prescribed some medicine and a hot bath. A hot bath was much easier said than done, since there was no running water. People had to fetch water from the nearest well, which was often a block or two away from one's house. The old, sick woman struggled to fill her galvanized bathtub, and then to bring the wood from the yard and build the fire to heat the water. These tasks took her half a day. About to step into the tub, she remembered the towel. She left the room to get it. When she returned, her husband was sitting in the bathtub.

She shouted at her husband, "What are you doing? The doctor said I must have a hot bath. I worked so hard. Why did you climb in? You know I am sick."

"I am sick, too," he answered.

Later she reached for her medicine. It was gone. "I used it up," her husband admitted. "I am sick, too." So she was left without a bath and without her medicine. The poor woman died.

At her funeral, her husband couldn't stop crying and talking about how much he loved his wife and how much he would miss her. He finished his long, tearful eulogy by saying, "Oy, Necha, Necha, you were so good. I will never forget you. Even after I remarry, I will never take your picture off the wall."

Another bittersweet tale served as the talk of the town for weeks. There was a Jewish shoemaker who couldn't earn a living to support his wife and six children. Day after day, he searched for work, desperately asking everybody for anything that could help his dire situation. He begged for a job, food, alms. He implored God for help — all to no avail. One day, an anti-Semitic Polish officer gave him a terrible beating. On top of the miseries that already burdened him, this pathetic, skinny, poverty-stricken man now had a permanent limp.

Afraid of being charged for the beating, which would have been a great embarrassment to him, the assaulting officer later sought out the shoemaker and gave him twenty zlotys. Seeing this as a sign from God, the unfortunate shoemaker became ecstatic — he thought he could now provide the essentials for his family. He told the whole town about his windfall. But before long, he realized that the twenty zlotys were not enough. Soon he was heard crying, "Where can I find another officer to beat me up for another twenty zlotys?" Even though the townspeople saw this as a tragic tale, the shoemaker's ridiculous plea made them laugh.

Though Jews and gentiles did intermingle well on a personal level, there still existed the usual institutional inequities that made Jews vulnerable to the gentile population. For example, no Jews in Lenin were allowed to hold public positions. As a result, Jews were generally intimidated when they needed to visit a government office and talk to the bureaucrats in charge.

Once, a townsman named Lazar Rabinovich needed a passport for his daughter. Without one, she could be arrested as an alien or a spy. Trembling with fear, he walked into the government building. He was confronted by an imposing man with whiskers seated in a large chair behind a huge desk. The official boomed out, "What do you want?" Rabinovich told him. "What is your name?" Rabinovich managed to tell him that, too. "And what is your daughter's name?" This was too much for Rabinovich. Sheer terror caused him to lose his voice and to forget his daughter's name! As he turned back towards the door, he murmured to the official, "Just a minute ..." and ran home. As soon as he saw his wife, he cried out, "Chaya, Chaya, what is our Luba's name?" Realization set in; he returned to the passport office. News of this incident spread quickly.

When a guest came from America to visit a Jewish relative in Lenin, the whole town celebrated together. The visitor was taken everywhere: to the river, the bridge, the hospital, the huge army barracks, and to the magnificent orchards. Formal greetings were given in front of each of the two synagogues and parties were thrown for the entire community. And when it was time for the guest to depart, the entire community would accompany the visitor to the coach to say farewell. On these occasions, the whole town became one big family.

Chapter Two

MY FAMILY

*J*T WAS A TIME in Eastern Europe when life revolved around
the home and ours was no exception. We were a very
close-knit family — my parents, myself and my six siblings.
The fact that we did not have extended family in Lenin
brought us even closer. It was natural to us to help each other
and sacrifice for each other; we didn't even give it a thought.
As we children grew older, we all contributed to supporting
the family.

We lived in a large rambling house which our father had
built. It had three entrances — one for our private use, one
for the restaurant my mother ran and one for the photo studio which existed in our home from time to time.

Our backyard was cluttered with small structures. There
was a small cottage which functioned as an icebox — the
only one in town — insulated with straw to keep the big
blocks of ice frozen throughout the hot summer days. We
also had a barn for the cow which gave us our daily milk and
for the horse loaned to my father for his business travels while
he was a salesman of sewing machines and spinning wheels. A
rickety shed stood behind the house, storage for the various
products my father sold, as well as for grain and corn for our
own use. As children, we loved our crowded backyard and

played amongst the tumbledown structures.

My father, Yakov Lazebnik, was born in the town of Motol near the city of Pinsk, around the year 1887. Motol was also the birthplace of Chaim Weizmann, who became the first president of the State of Israel. Weizmann happened to be a relative. When my parents were married, they settled in Lenin, where my mother had been born and raised.

My mother, Rayzel Migdalovich, often told us that as a young woman she had been introduced to many eligible young men, but she was very particular. For example, she rejected one potential groom because he held his spoon and mixed the sugar into his tea in a most peculiar way. Table manners were very important to her.

My father, on the other hand, she considered exceptional. She liked him instantly. He was learned and devout, came from a good family, had lovely manners, and was very charming, sensitive and kind. He was also handsome. When he proposed to my mother, she became the envy of all the girls.

My father used to say, "There are two kinds of people in this world: givers and takers. Since I am not a taker, I have to be a giver." And he gave — often more than he could afford.

Before I was born and when I was a very young child, our family was fairly well off. My parents owned a large fabric store so crammed with merchandise the existing shelves didn't suffice. The fabric was often piled in the middle of the store as high as a haystack.

Though both my parents worked very hard in the store, eventually they were no longer able to make a living at it. The major problem was my father's generous nature — he was generous to a fault. When poor people came to his store, lamenting that their children were starving and begging him for a few metres of fabric with which to barter for food, my father could not refuse. He would even, at times, cut more

*Faye's parents: Rayzel (Migdalovich) Lazebnik
and Yakov Lazebnik.*

fabric than they asked for, all the while knowing he would never be paid. This generous and impractical practice went on for years. At the end there was nothing left in the store but empty shelves.

My father then tried his hand at several other businesses, for which he had to borrow money. For a while, he sold Singer sewing machines and spinning wheels, travelling by horse and buggy in the countryside with his wares. But too often he sold these machines on credit to people who could not afford to pay for them. Again he lost money and was unable to pay off his debts. My father was honest and charitable; but the resulting reality was that he was a failed businessman who could not provide for his own family. We, his family, loved him nonetheless.

My father took his business failures in stride. He devoted himself to the synagogue and the Jewish community, which he served with pride. He was born a *kohan*, the priestly designation carried patrilineally, which gave him automatic prestige in the religious community, a prestige which was carried over into communal life. He was chosen as one of three dignitaries in the town who acted as arbitrators for the *bet din*. If there was a dispute in the Jewish community, rather than taking it to civil court, the community would organize the *bet din*, its own autonomous court. Only a citizen who was trusted as honourable and reliable by the whole town could act as a judge in these hearings. My father was one of the chosen few, along with the rabbi.

The community's high regard for my father also meant that he was elected president of the communal Jewish loan society. These societies were established to help Jewish entrepreneurs start new businesses. The Lenin Jewish Loan Society soon ran out of funds because my charitable, impractical father gave the money to the poor, rather than to the business people for whom it was meant. The community respected my father so much that they closed their eyes to this small problem.

All his adult life, my father worked as the *gabbe*, the official who takes care of synagogue business, in our synagogue. It was an unpaid position which included responsibility for the synagogue's meagre finances, paying the staff (the rabbi, cantor and beadle), organizing the building's maintenance and repairs, ordering supplies and giving alms to the poor on behalf of the congregation. Here my father was more successful — there was never much money involved.

Those who devoted themselves selflessly to religious life were often poor. My father's best friend was the rabbi, Rabbi Moishe Milshtein, with whom he spent many hours studying and discussing Torah. The rabbi's own meagre earnings were augmented by his wife's small business: selling yeast and candles to the community.

Another responsibility of the *gabbe* was to welcome Jewish guests to our town and find them lodging and food at no charge. This was in keeping with the Jewish precept that, according to the teachings of the Torah, regards hospitality as an important obligation. Whenever a visiting Jew found himself stranded in Lenin on the Sabbath, or any other holiday, he would be directed to our house. Rather than finding a place for the traveller with a wealthy Jewish family, as was the custom, my father would invite him to stay for dinner and the night in our home.

I remember the many pleasant hours our family spent extending such hospitality to our guests, especially on the Sabbath. Our guest would receive a place of honour at our dinner table. The crisp white tablecloth was laden with the best food our family could afford, expertly cooked by my mother. After breakfast the next morning, my father would take the visitor to the synagogue for prayers. The visitor was assigned a special seat and given additional honours during the service.

The whole family appreciated, and respected, my father's devotion to the Jewish community. We admired him immensely. The fact that he could not support us was not a concern to us. As we grew older, we were all happy to contribute financially to the family as we best could. We did so with the same devotion my parents had extended towards us in other ways.

As each child was born and our family grew, my parents became more and more poor. It was my mother who spent most of her time and energy at making a living. This was not unusual in Jewish households of the time. In those days it was considered *yiches*, an honour, for the man of the house to devote himself to religious study and prayer. The woman of the house accepted her role in dealing with all the practical aspects of household and livelihood.

My father devoted more and more time to the synagogue. Accordingly, my mother took over both the household and its financial support. She worked hard and for very long hours each day. When I close my eyes and try to picture my mother, I see her working in the kitchen: chopping, baking and presiding over immense pots. She was an excellent cook. When financial difficulties demanded it of her, she opened a restaurant in our home to augment the family income. The restaurant attracted many Polish officers who loved her cooking and came from miles around to eat at her table.

My mother was devoted to us. She worked very hard to bring up her seven children in a poor but well-kept home. She taught us loyalty to each other and respect for other people. She instilled in us a strong family ethic and a great love for Judaism. The whole family ate breakfast and dinner together every day around our large table. Our Friday night Sabbath meal, to which we all looked forward, was the highlight of our week. It held a warmth and sense of belonging that has remained with me for my whole life.

My mother also tended to the practical and social aspects of our lives; she wanted us to dress well and to practise proper table manners. She always wanted us to have friends from good homes. She herself liked to dress in the latest style. She was the disciplinarian in our family and we were afraid to cross her. But she was also very fun-loving and sociable. She liked good company and could carry on a lively conversation with anyone.

My mother had a sister and brother in America. We often received parcels from her sister Yetta. My mother loved the hand-me-down dresses which her sister sent. To my mother, they were the latest style and they made her feel very elegant.

At one point, my mother wrote her brother telling him

The Lazebnik family, mid-1930s. Back row, left to right: Faye,
Sonia, Moishe, Esther. Middle row: Yakov, Yakov's brother, Rayzel.
Front row: Boruch, Grainom. Kopel had already left Lenin to
pursue his religious studies at yeshiva.

that she would like to bring our family to America and asking
him to sponsor her. He answered: "My dear sister, in America
people must work very hard. You are not so strong. America is
not for you." Obviously he was wrong about my mother and
knew nothing about her life. Nor did he realize at the time
that he had tragically missed a chance to save many lives.

To us, our parents were holy. We were obedient children,
asking few questions and rarely questioning their authority.
This was the way of the world at the time. We felt very much
loved by our parents. I believe it was this love that gave me
the security and the resources that served me well later in my
life. Observing my mother's competence, my father's loving
nature, gave me the independence and personal strength that
helped me to survive in my gravest moments.

My mother had her children two years apart: three girls —
myself, Sonia and Esther; and four boys — Moishe, Kopel,
Grainom and Boruch. My eldest brother, the firstborn, was
Moishe. While my younger brothers were very religious,
Moishe was more interested in Zionism than in religion. Jews
were not allowed to attend university for higher professional
training. Since the professions were closed, my parents wanted Moishe to practise a skilled trade. He chose photography.
The closest large centre with a school for photography was
Pinsk, the capital of western White Russia. My parents had to
borrow the money to pay his tuition.

After Moishe learned his trade, he opened a photo studio
in our house in Lenin. He went to nearby villages and took
many photos of the Polish soldiers. Soon it was Moishe who
helped support the whole family. We all helped him develop
and print the photos at home. I remember spending hours in
the darkroom as a young girl, developing negatives.

When Moishe married, he left home and moved to
another town, Sienkevich, where he opened a photo studio.
My parents sent me to work for him in Sienkevich, because
he needed the help. While continuing to live in Sienkevich,
Moishe opened a second studio in Luniniec. I was only sixteen, but I was soon left to operate the new business in
Luniniec.

Working for my brother was not easy. Too often he
ordered me about and treated me like his little sister, which of
course I was. Yet, at the age of sixteen, I had assumed the
adult responsibilities of managing a business. I did it surpris-
ingly well. My clients were happy with my work because I
tried to show them in the best light. I studied their faces

before I took their photos, wanting to make them seem alive in their portraits. I stayed in Luniniec working as a photographer until the outbreak of the war.

Sonia was the eldest girl in our family. She worked as a secretary for the town's only lawyer, who was blind. Sonia also helped my parents financially. Though she was outwardly quiet, she was also very sociable and had many friends. She was the one to whom all her friends came with their secrets because she was wise and could be trusted to keep them confidential.

Everyone was astonished when Sonia became engaged to Yitzhak Koziolek, a rabbi. Her bridegroom came from Lodz and had studied at the Mezerich Yeshiva, the most orthodox

Faye's eldest sister Sonia and her husband, Rabbi Yitzhak Koziolek.

religious talmudic seminary in Poland. It was a match made by our brother Kopel who was a student at the Mezerich Yeshiva at the time. People wondered why Sonia would want to marry a rabbi and submit herself to so many religious restrictions. Marrying a rabbi meant she would have to change her way of life. She would be required to wear modest clothing and a *sheytl,* the obligatory wig worn by very religious Jewish women. No longer could she go to the cinema to see the films that she loved. And in her household she would have to adhere to the strict kosher requirements prescribed by the rabbis. Even though we were observant, we were not used to these strict restrictions in our childhood home.

When Sonia's bridegroom came to visit Lenin just before their marriage, he gave an impressive speech in our synagogue and immediately became the talk of the town. It was then that everyone realized what an honour it would be to have such a learned husband. Everyone said it was a good match after all.

After their wedding, Sonia joined her husband in Lubartov, a town near Lublin. Sonia's husband had become head of his own yeshiva. When I was fourteen, my mother sent me to live with Sonia for six months. I would be able to help with the constant flow of guests and boarders that Sonia had staying at her home, all of whom were associated with the yeshiva.

This was before I worked for my brother Moishe in Luniniec; it was my first time away from home. How different life was outside of Lenin! For one thing, in Lubartov I encountered blatant anti-Semitism for the first time. One Saturday afternoon, as I was walking on a crowded sidewalk with two girlfriends, I suddenly felt a burning sensation in my eyes. A young Polish boy had purposely flung some kind of powder at us and the powder had been sprayed in my eyes. My friends, both from *Bais Yakov*, a religious girls' school, were dressed in the school uniform, so we were recognizable as Jewish girls. For the moment I was blinded. I was led by my friends to the closest door, which opened into a small store. The storekeeper let me wash out my eyes. My face swelled up and my eyes were red for a week.

This was my first anti-Semitic encounter, but not my last.

In another incident one morning, I had gone to the well near our house only to find pieces of pork floating in the water. Whoever threw them in knew that this well was used by the Jews from the nearby seminary. Since Jews are not allowed to eat pork, they had rendered the water useless to us.

Despite these incidents, I was happy in my sister's home. Her house was very warm and pleasant and always filled with people from the yeshiva. They all had the utmost respect for my brother-in-law, who was the *rosh*, or the head, of the yeshiva. Every day at dinnertime, yeshiva teachers and students gathered round, telling jokes, chanting blessings, singing religious songs after every meal. It was a very joyous as well as religious atmosphere and I was very deeply affected by my experience there. I learned the grace after meals by heart and said prayers three times daily. In the atmosphere of my sister and brother-in-law's home, I became much more deeply religious than ever before.

I helped my sister cook and serve meals to all the guests and helped with the numerous household chores. In return, she and her husband arranged for me to attend private art lessons given by a Jewish art teacher in his studio. I was one of four students who came every day to learn art photography and painting. I was taught to tint black-and-white pictures — there were no colour photographs at the time — and I studied design, colour and perspective. Having an artistic bent, I thoroughly enjoyed my six months of training while I lived with my sister and used it to my benefit in all my future work.

❦

My brother Kopel, the third eldest child, was clever, determined and as good-natured as our father. If he wanted to do something, nothing could hold him back. He decided to study Torah. In Lenin there were no yeshivas, so my parents sent him to Pinsk. An ardent student, he studied day and night. He didn't want to rent an apartment because he didn't think there would be time to go home and sleep. Instead, he slept on a bench beside his religious books.

My parents worried about Kopel's health. Although we hardly had enough for ourselves, my mother managed to send him parcels of food regularly. We later found out he gave these parcels away to the hungry boys studying with him. Malnourished, he became ill. My parents wanted him to come home, but the rabbis wouldn't allow it; they sent him to a resort to recover. Instead of resting, my brother organized a yeshiva at the spa, urging boys to learn Talmud. Again he had no rest.

Kopel then transferred to the most religious talmudic academy in Poland, the Mezerich Yeshiva. The rabbis quickly recognized his ardour and genius. They wanted to keep him there. When my mother wrote Kopel a letter asking him to come home for the holidays, he refused. The rabbis did not want to release him, since they were afraid that his parents might not let him return. Again my parents worried about Kopel's health. One day, my mother decided to go to Mezerich and bring him home, hoping to send him to a less rigorous school.

46

When she arrived at Mezerich, the rabbis would not allow her to see him. My mother was livid. She pounded the table with her fists, crying and threatening to call the police. The rabbis told her to go back home; they would let Kopel come home for the holidays. Heart-broken, she returned to Lenin without seeing her son. True to their word, the rabbis sent Kopel home for the holidays.

This time my father said, "Enough is enough. You can study the Torah, but not in that yeshiva; it's too Orthodox. You'll go to the Baranovich Yeshiva. Our rabbi knows the head of the yeshiva there. You'll get a good recommendation." Kopel did not protest.

My father took him to the train station, bought him a ticket to Baranovich, and came home feeling he had accomplished something. "Thank God, now maybe Kopel will change, and he won't be a *mussarnic*, a mystic, any more. He will be able to enjoy life, too."

In the meantime, Kopel had boarded the train, disembarked at the next stop, changed his ticket, and gone back to Mezerich. My parents gave up. They knew that there was nothing more they could do.

A few years passed. It was time for Kopel to enter the Polish army for compulsory military service. He became a top marksman and a good soldier, so good that the captain let him go to the closest synagogue every Sabbath. Of course Kopel remained religious; the local rabbi arranged for him to have kosher meals every day. But when manoeuvres started and he had to be in the field, no kosher food was available. Kopel didn't eat and became very weak. When he finally collapsed, he was taken to a hospital. Upon his release from hospital, he managed to complete his military service and obtain an honourable discharge. Afterwards, he returned to Mezerich.

In 1939 when war broke out and Poland was divided between the Soviet Union and Germany, Mezerich fell under Nazi occupation. Jews were expelled and Kopel came back to Lenin where he continued his studies with our local Rabbi Milshtein.

❧

My sister Esther was beautiful. She was only eighteen months older than I. She had blond wavy hair, which was uncommon for a Jewish girl. I envied her beauty and resented the extra care my mother gave her. She was frail, always catching colds and coughing. My mother attributed her frailness to a severe bout of pneumonia which Esther had suffered as a child.

I felt that Esther was treated like a queen by my mother. Though she was older, I was the one who had to do all the work in the house: cleaning, washing the floors, bringing water from the well, going to the market and helping my mother in the kitchen. At the time I didn't appreciate it, but my mother was right. I was stronger and healthier than my sister and therefore it was appropriate that I should do the heavy work.

My jealousy towards Esther subsided as I became older and more confident. At an annual dance given by the Jewish community in Luniniec, where I was working for my brother Moishe, I was chosen the Queen of the Ball. In my red chiffon dress, which I had sewn myself for the occasion, I felt beautiful for the first time in my life. In reality, I was probably given this title because I was considered a guest in town, but my newly won title built up my confidence and made me feel that I probably wasn't so bad looking after all. From then on, my resentment eased whenever I heard people saying how beautiful Esther was.

In spite of my petty jealousy, Esther and I had always been good friends. Since we were close in age, we had many friends in common. We often went to dances and other social functions together. She was an excellent student, while I had little patience for my studies. Because she was so good-natured, she often took pity on me and helped me with my homework.

Most of all, my sister Esther and I had many laughs together. I had a boyfriend in another town whom I had met in Sienkevich at the time I was working there for my brother Moishe. In the heat of courtship, he wrote letters to me every day. Because I hated to write, I asked Esther to write him back in my name. He never knew the truth. This correspondence lasted for many months, much to our mutual amusement.

Esther married Meyer Feldman, a tall, handsome young man from Pinsk who came to Lenin in 1939 during the Soviet occupation. He was one of the two doctors in residence at the hospital. At that time, Esther worked in the hospital as a secretary. Esther and her doctor met, fell in love and were married.

⚘

I remember my brother Grainom as a very handsome boy, two years younger than I was. I saw little of Grainom because he was seldom home. In the morning he went to Polish school. Then he rushed home, had a bite to eat, did his homework and hurried off to *cheder* to study Torah.

In 1939, when the Soviets took over our town, Torah study was forbidden. Grainom left for Vilna, then in Lithuania, to continue his studies in a yeshiva. My parents were worried about a thirteen-year-old away from home in a strange country. They asked my father's family in the United States to sponsor Grainom in America. When the postcard confirming the necessary arrangements finally arrived, it was too late. Jews were no longer allowed to leave Nazi-occupied territory. Later my brother Grainom, who had stayed at the yeshiva in Vilna, became another martyr in the long list of Lithuanian yeshiva rabbis and students murdered by the Nazis.

My youngest brother, Boruch, whom I loved the most, was an innocent, soft-spoken boy who was everyone's favourite. Sometimes, because he was so quiet, we couldn't tell whether he was even in the house. When the Nazis occupied our town, twelve year old Boruch was put to forced labour. He worked very hard on a dairy farm where milk was made into butter and cheese. He never complained. He was so proud when he brought his weekly "pay" to the ghetto every Friday. It was a bottle of *peregon*, the sour water squeezed out from yogurt to make cheese. Before the war, my mother gave *peregon* to our cow. But Boruch was proud of his earnings, and all of us were proud of him — with pain in our hearts and tears in our eyes.

Over fifty years have passed since my life with my beloved family was destroyed. I have tried to capture some semblance of our life together as I remember it before the Holocaust. The years that followed and the tragedy of their deaths are still a painful memory to me.

Chapter Three

UNDER SOVIET OCCUPATION

*O*N SEPTEMBER 1, 1939, the Nazis invaded Poland. Later that month, according to the secret agreement signed earlier between Hitler and Stalin, occupation of Poland was divided between Nazi Germany and the Soviet Union. For the time being, the Soviet Union assumed control of the eastern side of the country, and the Nazis occupied the western side. Poland, as we had known it, no longer existed. We found ourselves under Soviet rule.

Although our way of life was inevitably changed under communism, we still maintained a semblance of our old lives. And for most people in Lenin the result was quite tolerable. Since, under the communist regime, work was compulsory for everyone, most of the populace was employed. Wages were meagre, but people were somehow able to eke out a living. Under a regime that did not approve of religion, those who, like my father, kept religious observances had an especially difficult time finding work which would allow them to observe the Sabbath.

The few wealthy families in Lenin fared the worst. The Soviets regarded them as capitalists and therefore exploiters of the people, and all were summarily thrown into prison or exiled to Siberia. The government seized their businesses and personal possessions. Having lost our business several years earlier, my own family was not targeted. Ironically, exile to Siberia might have preserved, and not destroyed our lives.

My sister and I attended evening classes to learn Russian, since Russian had now become the official language. We knew it would be useful for our work. Having returned from Luniniec at the outbreak of the war, I continued to work as a photographer in the studio in my parents' home. My experience in my brother's business, as well as the classes in painting and art photography that my sister Sonia had encouraged me to take while I lived with her, were now serving me well. I had a successful profession and earned a surprising amount of money.

After a whole day spent taking pictures, I turned my handful of rubles over to my father without even bothering to count them. I saw that he was grateful and gladly gave him all my earnings. My father had been forced to borrow money to make ends meet. Now he could begin to honour his debts. I was happy and proud to contribute to my family's income. It made me into a responsible adult at a very young age. I felt very important in my newly found maturity.

The Soviets decreed that every individual in the occupied territory must have a passport with a photo. Consequently, I had no shortage of work and encountered all kinds of people in the process. To some, photography was nothing less than wizardry. Peasants who had never been to school nor ever left their homes appeared without notice in my photo studio. Once I handed a mirror to a new client and instructed him to brush his hair. The peasant stared at himself in the mirror. Then he glanced up at me and exclaimed in confusion, "Who is that? He looks much like me." This man knew how he looked only from his reflection in the river or in a pail of water: he had never seen his own image in a mirror.

There were difficult as well as amusing moments. I was ordered to take passport pictures in a town called Mikashevich, eighteen kilometres from home. By the time I finished my work it was late and the coachman who had brought me had already left. I had no way of getting back and had to wait until morning. Night was falling. No hotel was available and I knew no one in town. I decided to spend the night in the train station where it was warm. I wore a coat with pockets jammed full of passports and film, and my camera was slung over my shoulder. Exhausted, I stretched out on a hard station bench. Despite my best efforts to stay awake, I nodded off for several hours.

In the morning, the coachman arrived and together we set out for Lenin. When I got home, I emptied out my coat pockets and noticed that there was one passport missing. Most likely it had fallen out of my pocket while I had slept in the train station. At first I was not alarmed, unaware of the possible implications and consequences of such a loss. I was still learning about the new Soviet laws. But I soon realized I myself could be accused of confiscating the passport and might be considered a spy. Spying was a common charge in the Soviet Union; many people were arrested and sent to Siberia on suspicion of spying. As the seriousness of the situation dawned on me, I became afraid.

In the next few days, after the authorities found out about the missing passport, I began to notice a change in attitude when Soviet officials encountered me on the street. I was accustomed to being greeted pleasantly on the streets of Lenin by members of the NKVD, the National Commissariat of Internal Affairs and predecessor of the KGB. Now they were avoiding me. I surmised that I might be a candidate for Siberia.

Luckily, after four anxious days, somebody found the missing passport and handed it over to the police. I was cleared of suspicion and soon the friendly greetings of the Soviet officials resumed.

As a citizen of an occupied territory, I felt especially vulnerable. There were a number of Russians stationed in our town who wished to have pictures taken privately for their own pleasure, but few could afford this on their meagre salaries. They came to me anyway and owed me the money. As a result they began to resent me. I had fears that they might want me deported to Siberia. Sensing their growing animosity and their power over me, I began to tell each Russian whom I suspected was unwilling to pay, "Don't worry, it is my gift to you. You don't have to pay me." They appreciated this and thanked me. In the end, such people became my friends.

In the summer of 1940, after I had been working very hard for about a year, my health began to deteriorate. I had frequent fevers, sore throats and colds. My mother took me to the doctor, who informed us that my tonsils had to be removed by a surgeon. I would have to go to Pinsk for the operation.

My mother took me to Pinsk and my first experience in a hospital. The hospital was an enormous building whose interior appeared completely white and sterile. For me at the time, it was frightening. As the nurse led me away, I turned back to look at my mother. Her look of worry and distress made me want to cry. Weeks later, I could barely recall the pain of the operation, but the memory of my mother's face remained clear.

Four days after the operation, I was discharged from the hospital. My mother and I took the train from Pinsk to Mikashevich and planned to take a horse and wagon for the eighteen kilometre journey back to Lenin. However, as soon as we stepped out from the train, we were met by several

Soviet officers, who lost no time in telling us that sixty army majors were waiting for me to take their passport photographs. They had all come to Mikashevich expressly to await my arrival.

My throat was still in excruciating pain, and I was not yet able to speak. I wrote in Russian on a piece of paper that I had just had an operation, that I couldn't talk and that I didn't even have my camera with me. "Don't worry," they replied. "We've already thought of this. We've brought you your camera. We got it from your father. Take our photographs, and we'll transport you and your mother home in our car."

Silently, motioning as articulately as possible with my hands, I took pictures of all sixty Soviet officers. Afterwards, they drove me and my mother home. Only the army had cars at that time. No civilian could afford to own one. I was thankful that I didn't have to travel eighteen kilometres by horse and wagon on those rough roads; it would have shaken my throat to pieces.

⌘

It was Friday night. My mother had lit the Sabbath candles, and my father had just come home from the synagogue. The whole family was sitting at the table, and my mother was ready to serve supper. The candles in the polished shining silver candlesticks illuminated the table and the *challahs* were draped with a beautiful embroidered cover on the opposite side of the table. Father said the blessings over the food we were about to eat. Everyone was experiencing the holy Sabbath, our day of rest.

Suddenly, there was a knock at the door. My father answered it, and was confronted by a Soviet officer who wanted his picture taken. I told him, "I am sorry. I don't take pictures on the Sabbath. This is our holiday and we are not allowed to work today."

The officer insisted that he must have his passport photo immediately. "I have come from sixty kilometres away," he announced. "And I was told that there is a photographer here." Requests for passport photos were always phrased in the most urgent tones.

I answered emphatically, "I cannot help you tonight. I do not take pictures on the Sabbath." I was determined not to work on the Sabbath even if it cost me my life. Such was my youthful stubbornness.

In the face of my implacability, the officer resorted to scare tactics. He threaten to report me to the NKVD. I remained steadfast in my position. After this argument had gone on for a while, I looked over at my father and saw that he was upset. He could not tell me to obey, nor could he advise me not to. Eventually, the Soviet officer left, and my father burst into tears. In a breaking voice, he declared, "Now, my daughter, I can die peacefully. I know that you will remain a good Jew. It is written in the book of Exodus, 'Remember the Sabbath day, to keep it holy' and you have obeyed."

Though we were becoming used to such disruptions in our daily lives, Soviet-occupied Poland still felt relatively safe for Jews. At the same time, Jews were fleeing western Nazi-occupied Poland in the thousands. During the winter of 1940/41, the new border between Soviet-occupied and Nazi-occupied Poland was not yet completely closed, and escape was possible though difficult.

Many Jewish refugees from the west arrived in our town. Having left their homes and often even their families, they now found themselves without food, shelter or work. As we had no extra beds to offer these refugees, my father spread straw on the floor in every room in the house, opened the door and declared, "Anyone who doesn't have a place to sleep is welcome. This house is open to all." Consequently, our home was always filled with people, who slept wherever they could find a place on the floor.

My mother served meals to all. Many guests lodged with us for a long time, while others stayed only briefly before travelling further east into the Soviet Union. They all spoke of how bad conditions were in western Poland under the Nazis.

My parents were terribly concerned about my sister Sonia, who lived in Nazi-occupied western Poland. They expected Sonia and her two infants to join us in Lenin for safety. Among the many refugees streaming through Lenin, there was no sign of Sonia. Imagining that Sonia might be among the refugees detained at the border of Nazi- and Soviet-occupied Poland at Brest-Litovsk, my parents sent me there to search for her. Perhaps Sonia had run out of money and she and the children were hungry.

My mother packed a few days' supply of food for me and I set off to Brest-Litovsk. Once I arrived, I was thrust into a frantic crowd which shoved me roughly from all directions. The station was overcrowded with families who had become separated and were searching for each other. I saw elderly people, young mothers with babies, and men and children of all ages, all looking frightened and haggard, frantically calling the names of their loved ones. I pushed through the crowds, looking for my sister in this crush of humanity.

I had no luck. All the faces belonged to strangers. At one end of the station, I noticed a Soviet soldier assembling a group of refugees. I realized that they were being sent back over the border to Nazi-occupied Poland. The Soviet government did not encourage the sheltering of refugees. When Soviet soldiers caught people crossing the border, they sent them back west.

Apprehensive, I steered my way to the opposite end of the building. Everywhere displaced and dispirited people sat or lay on the cold floor. I felt a wild impulse to run away, as far as possible. But, after having come so far, how could I go home empty-handed? I sat down on the floor to compose myself, and took some bread and cheese from the package my mother had given me. A small boy sitting nearby eyed me intently as I ate. He did not utter a word, but I could read his eyes. I pitied him; he was much younger than I and was obviously hungry. I broke off a large chunk of bread and a piece of cheese for him. He said only, "Thank you very much." As he ate, his eyes grew calmer. When he had finished his modest meal, he moved closer to his mother, who was sleeping beside him, closed his eyes and fell asleep.

I rose and half-heartedly resumed my search. I felt helpless, on the verge of tears, but I was unwilling to give up. From time to time, I peeked behind coats and blankets at the faces, but no sign of Sonia. Meanwhile, night had fallen, and the train station's interior was dimly lit, complicating my task still further. Overwhelmed with fatigue, I found an empty space on the floor and fell asleep.

For four days, I wandered through the throngs of refugees, peering into thousands of faces. Newcomers were constantly arriving. I was disappointed and exhausted, and no longer expected to find my sister. In addition, I had used up the last of my provisions, and was hungry and thirsty. Finally, I had to admit defeat.

Disgusted with myself for having failed, I returned home in tears. My mother tried to comfort me. "Don't worry," she said stoically. "We won't give up. Now it's Kopel's turn to go. We must bring Sonia home." Kopel, who was four years older than I, interrupted his Torah studies to look for Sonia.

Kopel also did not succeed in finding Sonia at the station

in Brest-Litovsk. Knowing how bitterly this would disappoint my mother, he decided to cross the Bug River into Nazi Poland and travel to Lubartov. Perhaps Sonia had never left home at all.

This was a dangerous and costly undertaking. The farmers who illegally escorted Jews across the river charged exorbitant rates to ferry refugees at night. The short journey was fraught with peril. If the Soviets spotted such a boat, they ordered the people to turn back; if they refused, the Soviets would shoot. Kopel resolved not to pay for his border crossing; instead, he pushed himself into a group of refugees whom the Soviets were throwing back into Nazi-occupied Poland. He was soon on the other side of the border.

As he had expected, Sonia was still at home. Her husband could not bring himself to disband the school. He felt strongly that, as long as his students remained, it was his duty to study Torah with them. Teaching Torah was all important to him. His goal now was to reach Vilna, where religious study was still allowed, and he planned to send for his wife and children later. It was decided that Kopel should accompany Sonia, her three year old son and one year old daughter to her family in Lenin. Sonia's husband remained in Lubartov where he was eventually killed by the Nazis.

The journey back to Lenin was arduous and took an entire week. When they arrived home to Lenin, my mother immediately threw herself into the task of restoring the children to health. They were ill, dirty and covered with lice. Leah, my one year old niece, had her magnificent gold curls shorn in order to rid her of parasites. Under my mother's loving care, the two children soon recovered and thrived.

Sonia was able to maintain contact with her husband. We were all increasingly concerned about him. Many other residents of Lenin also corresponded with relatives and friends on the other side of the border. The letters we received contained no news which would give rise to alarm. For the moment, it seemed that the inhabitants of Nazi-occupied Poland who had chosen to stay continued to conduct their daily lives much as before.

One day, the Soviets announced that whoever wished to return to Nazi-occupied territory should register. Refugees were thrown into a dreadful dilemma. Many were tired of running. In eastern Poland, they had no permanent place to live, they couldn't speak Russian, and they had no means of employment. Families had been painfully divided. Some had left parents behind; others had left wives, sisters and brothers. Thousands of people, relying on reports that the situation was not as bad in western Poland as they had been led to believe, registered to return.

My sister had to decide whether to stay or return. None of us felt competent to advise her. We discussed her situation endlessly; she longed to be with her husband. In the end, she decided not to register. She simply stated, "I'm tired of running. Here I know my children and I have a home." My parents were pleased with her decision.

They were doubly relieved when they learned that the Soviets had played a trick. Citing the classic Russian maxim, *Khto nyeh snameh tot protchev nas* [who is not with us is against us] — meaning that anyone who would rather be a German subject than a Soviet subject was considered an enemy — they dispatched all the registrants to Siberia rather than westward to their homes as they had promised. We saw thousands of people herded onto trains departing in the wrong direction, and later we received letters with Siberian return addresses.

At the time, the fate of these individuals was regarded as tragic. My sister, like everyone else who had decided to stay, was enormously relieved. No one could have foreseen that, ironically, Siberia would be the safest place for a Jew. Regardless of the hardships, Jews were able to survive in Siberia, since the Nazi rule never extended that far east. In fact, it was impossible to make a truly informed decision. Today, I wish that my whole family had registered.

Chapter Four

THE NAZI REIGN OF TERROR

*O*N JUNE 22, 1941, Nazi forces attacked Soviet-occupied Poland and the Soviet Union. That night, a strange commotion woke me up. Something was going on outside. The noise sounded closer and closer. Our whole family was up now. We looked through the windows, not turning on the lights inside the house.

We were met by a terrible sight. Countless people were walking in the middle of the street, chained by their feet to one another. They were emaciated, their faces pinched with pain. Because the moon was shining brightly, I could see them clearly, about four feet from the window. I watched them drag themselves along with what seemed like their last few ounces of strength. Their clothes were torn pieces of rags hanging from them. They were bent over, almost to the waist, hardly able to lift their chained feet. From time to time, someone fell. Immediately, he would be hit by a guard and then raise himself up to continue walking.

Except for the clatter of the chains, deathly quiet reigned. It took a long time until all of them — hundreds at least — passed by. We didn't say a word; it was painful enough to watch. With our heads down, we went back to our beds.

The next morning we found out that they were prisoners

evacuated from the Soviet jail in Pinsk and being sent east, deeper into the Soviet Union. The Soviets had anticipated their own defeat and decided to move their prisoners. The only crime committed by some of these prisoners had been to own a store; this made them exploiters and enemies of communism.

For the first time, I felt the penetrating bitterness and horror of war. Little did I know there was far worse to come.

Two days later, on June 24, the Nazi army occupied our town without resistance. The Soviets had left in panic two days earlier. Their non-aggression pact with the Nazis, which had ended abruptly with the Nazi invasion, along with other factors, had rendered the Soviet government unprepared for war. The Soviet Union's twenty-one month rule over our town was over. The Soviets were disorganized and only had time to dismantle their government and evacuate their prisoners.

For two days, our usually well-guarded town was completely without rule. The Jewish population was afraid of a pogrom. Knowing there was no one to stop them, the peasants from outside the town were ready to raid and plunder Jewish homes. They came into town with big sacks which they hoped to fill with stolen booty. As the situation grew tense, the Jewish youth organized themselves and were on guard day and night. Though the Jewish patrol had no guns, the peasants knew they were being watched, and they hesitated. Soon it was too late. Within two days, the Nazis swept into town with their tanks, heavy artillery and large battalions of soldiers. The anti-Semitic peasants had lost their chance.

Nazi forces moved continuously eastward into the Soviet Union, unimpeded. To enter Russia, they had to cross over our bridge in Lenin across the Sluch River. Our town once again became the focal point for military activity. Day and night, Nazi army detachments marched through town. En route, they invaded homes and took whatever they wanted. They especially liked to pull silk dresses from closets and tear them up for scarves which they wore as trophies around their military collars.

Now the real terror began for us. The Nazis began to implement their of persecution of the Jews. The Jewish population of Lenin, which had been so insulated from anti-Semitic activity, was immediately terrorized by the random atrocities and looting which followed the Nazis wherever they conquered. Nazi soldiers amused themselves by taking Jews to the cemetery and ordering them to dance around the tombstones. Time failing a trip to the cemetery, they ordered Jews to dance on the tables in their own homes. All this was encouraged by the Nazi command.

The difficulties for our family began early. We had a big house with three front doors. Those who had one front door had one set of Nazis coming in to loot. We had three. One night, we were roused by a pounding on one of our doors. We had to open; otherwise the Nazis would break the door down and shoot us. We knew this had already happened at other houses.

Two Nazis walked in and ordered my sister Esther and me to undress and face the wall. We stood next to each other against the wall, trembling, when she whispered to me, "They are going to shoot us." She continued to whisper her fears to me.

The two Nazis were standing behind us, pointing the rifles at our backs, shouting at us and swearing, "You dirty Jews! You have to be eliminated! You are dirty dogs!" I couldn't understand everything they shouted. All their yells mixed together in my ears until all I heard was one loud noise. I don't know what would have happened if two other Nazis had not rushed in to say they were late. The soldiers had to catch up with the rest of their brigade. They had no time to finish with us.

It is hard to explain my feelings at that time, standing with my sister against the wall. We had thought we were at death's door. In the morning, my body was covered in a rash of red spots. My brother-in-law the doctor said it was a nervous reaction.

We were all forced to work for the Nazis for no pay. At the beginning of the occupation, I was sent with a group of four or five Jewish girls to work in Nazi-occupied houses in Lenin. The Nazis demanded cleaning girls for their living quarters and offices. We were forced to scrub the wooden floors, peel potatoes, wash dishes and do their laundry by hand. We had to carry heavy buckets of water from the well and to polish their shoes. Often, we were beaten. I remember everyone was always shouting at us. When they were not satisfied with our work, it was worse. They shouted louder, and forced us to work faster and harder.

Although it was unpleasant and humiliating, there were some benefits to domestic work. When I had to clean up the tables from the parties of the previous night, there were often leftovers from their extravagant meals. Sometimes, we found bread on the floor under the table. Whenever I could, I took food home to my family. Access to food had become increasingly scarce and we often went hungry.

Each day, fifty to a hundred Jews were selected to work for the Nazi troops. They were forced to sweep the streets and roads, clean their horses, scrub floors and wash their underwear. For all of us, it was a hard day of forced labour without payment or food. When the light of day arrived, we begged for night when could go home to rest. At night, we prayed to go to work the next day, so frightened were we of being killed during the night.

During the first week of the Nazi invasion our family was roused one night by three Nazis with rifles. They shouted, "Up! Up! Into the kitchen!" Then, "Lie on the floor! Face down!" Laughing amongst themselves, they had fun looking at us lying speechless and frightened, waiting to be shot. They ordered us to sing. Frozen from fear, no one made a sound. One of the Nazis stopped laughing, became angry and shouted, "Sing or I will shoot!"

My brother Kopel, the yeshiva student, started to sing. He sang *Kaddish*, the mourner's prayer. We joined him, shaking with fear. My heart seemed to stop beating. I felt the pain of the bullet that was not yet in me. Was it the end this time?

Eventually, the Nazis left. The ordeal was over. We got up and stood silently for a long time as though glued to the kitchen floor, unable to move. We were all in shock. Slowly we started to move and went back to our beds for the night. Incidents like this became common occurrences.

After a few weeks, the traffic of thousands of Nazi soldiers marching to the front through Lenin stopped. By this time the front line was already several hundred kilometres east into the Soviet Union, well past our town. The town of Lenin was now placed under a permanent Nazi military government.

When the new Nazi government took over, I began my work as a photographer again. I was "employed" by the Nazis to process their photographs, a job for which I sometimes received some extra food. Otherwise, my work was part of the slave labour we Jews were forced to do. The Nazis were obsessed with documenting their activities and took many photographs. Often these photos showed Nazis taunting and killing Jews. Though I hated this work, I also knew it might

save my life. I soon gained a reputation for my coloured portraits as well, and was kept consistently busy.

In the process of my work, I met many Germans, hundreds, maybe thousands, as they passed through our town.
Out of all the Germans with whom I dealt, I recall only one
as being sympathetic. He was among the Germans stationed
in town. I processed a portrait of his wife and an enlargement
of a picture of his children. To develop the negatives, I needed lots of water. Every day and sometimes a couple of times
daily, I had to take the pail and go to the well. On the way, I
had to pass his office. This German watched me through the
window as I carried my heavy pail.

Although I worked like an adult, I was still a young girl,
thin and hungry. Once when I was going to the well with an
empty pail, he rushed out in front of me. He went to the
well, stopped for a moment and left very quickly in the other
direction. I was scared. I didn't know what he was doing.
When I arrived at the well, I was relieved to see that he had
left a piece of bread for me. I hid the bread in my pocket.
When I got home, I burst into tears and gave the bread to my
mother. He did this several times before he disappeared. I
later found out that this soldier was arrested for refusing to
obey an order to kill someone.

My experiences as a photographer were not always so
rewarding. On another occasion, a Nazi policeman walked in
and shouted that he wanted a passport picture right away —
in one hour. If it was not ready, he would make me "kaput."
He pulled his hand across his throat, indicating my demise. I
took his photo and tried to process it immediately. The problem was that the negative had to dry before it could be printed. I blew on it continuously, but it was still wet. The time
passed too quickly; there were only thirty minutes left and
the negative was still wet. I began to look through the bottles

in the house until I found a small bottle of alcohol. Quickly, I dipped the negative in and shook it a few times, then blew on it. The negative dried. Now I could make his prints.

The Nazi returned exactly one hour later. When I handed him his pictures, he was astonished. He looked at them, seemed to like them, but did not change his attitude. Again, he shouted at me, "You are lucky, you cursed Jew," and left. This was his show of appreciation.

With the permanent Nazi government in Lenin, the entire Jewish community faced increasing restrictions on our lives. One after the other new decrees against the Jews were issued. We had to wear yellow stars, front and back. We were no longer allowed to attend school, to travel or own business-es. It was decreed that Jews were not allowed to walk on the sidewalk. The streets became almost empty except for Nazi soldiers who patrolled with unleashed dogs. When the Nazis pointed to a Jew and shouted "*Jude!*" the dogs would attack and tear the person apart.

The Nazis also issued quotas to the Jews, demanding so many pairs of leather gloves, so many pillows, blankets, fur coats, gold watches, and so forth. The first fur coat they received belonged to my sister Sonia. Hostages were taken and the Nazis warned that they would be killed if the Nazis' orders were not fulfilled.

The Nazis established a Jewish council, called the *Judenrat*, whose members were hand-picked by the Nazis to expedite their orders. And the *Judenrat* was kept extremely busy. It was no longer a matter of one fur coat, or a gold watch, or a gold chain. Now there was an order that Jews were not allowed to own fur coats altogether. Not only fur coats, but every fur collar sewn on a cloth coat had to be cut off and given to the Nazis. My mother sat for hours cutting off the fur collars from all our coats.

Next, Jews were not allowed to own gold. Anything made out of gold was requisitioned by the Nazis: gold coins, watches, rings, chains, bracelets, brooches. These were things which Jews had used to trade for bread. Now there was nothing left to offer the farmers for food.

We had little food left in our house. The Nazis had already taken the cow, so there was no milk for the children. My mother was worried; we were eating sparsely. Her soups were now made with little more than flour and salt and the occasional potato added to water. There was no longer enough food to go around.

Random killings of Jews occurred daily. My father was among several Jews ordered to bury twelve Jewish teenagers who had been killed by the Nazis. My gentle father had never been able to deal with the sight of blood. I will never forget the anguished expression on his face when I accidentally cut myself while helping him chop wood. And here he would have to deal with bloodied dead bodies. Because he had no choice, he went to the site as he was told. As soon as he saw the lifeless victims lying in blood, he fainted. The others revived him and sent him home.

Another night, the Nazis led out fifteen boys to kill gratuitously. The defenceless youngsters were marched out with rifles pointed at them. They were warned that if one Nazi was harmed or killed, the Nazis would kill a hundred more Jews. On their way to the Nazis' favourite killing spot — the courtyard of the government buildings — the boys had to cross the small bridge over the lake dividing the old town and the new. One of the fifteen boys, Yitzhak Brodocky, decided not to give the Nazis the pleasure of killing him. Instead he jumped off the bridge into the lake. The other fourteen were shot.

The Nazis could not get over their embarrassment at allowing a Jew to escape. The next morning, they took four additional hostages: the rabbi, my father, and two other prominent men from our town. Hostages were always chosen according to their importance to the community. The Nazis believed in collective retaliation. If they were crossed by one Jew, the entire community would be punished. If Yitzhak were not found, the four would be killed.

We were all worried, especially my mother. Nobody knew where Yitzhak was. And even if someone had known, who would have told? Soon after, Yitzhak's body was found floating on the surface of the lake: he had been fatally injured in his jump from the bridge. The Nazis were pleased and my father and the other hostages were released.

Two particularly vicious Nazis often drove into Lenin by horse and wagon from a village about fifteen kilometres away. They came to rob and vandalize Jewish homes, often killing Jews who got in their way. At first we thought they were Nazi officials, but in fact they were Nazi paratroopers who had been dropped behind the Soviet front lines. Instead of returning to their unit, they stayed in the region to terrorize the Jewish population.

Whenever these two thugs appeared in town, everybody was too frightened to walk out in the street. The town was silent, people waiting, defenceless, for the ordeal to be over. With loaded rifles, these thugs walked into homes, turning everything upside down and taking whatever they wanted. If someone objected, he or she would be shot.

One day, an elderly Jewish woman came running to our door, crying and begging for the doctor, my brother-in-law, to come to her house. Her husband had been shot by the two Nazis who had demanded vodka and tobacco, but he was still alive. My brother-in-law suggested that they wait for the Nazis to leave town, but the woman insisted he come immediately. Knowing he was risking his own life, my brother-in-law left with her and tended to the wounded man. He came home shaking. "They have seen me," he told us. He feared what would happen now. The two hoodlums went back to the man's house and put three more bullets into him. Now they were sure that he was dead.

My brother Kopel told me that one of the two came into our house later that same day and stood him against the wall with his gun to Kopel's head. "Tell me who in town has guns or ammunition?" the Nazi demanded. Almost without thinking, my brother calmly answered, "A while back, the local government ordered all citizens to hand over guns and ammunition to the police and we all did so." The Nazi seemed satisfied with the answer and left.

Winter was coming and we were all very hungry. There was a wealthy old man in town, a gentile, who owned a lot of land. His potatoes were ready to be dug up. Feeling sorry for us, he told the Jews that they could help themselves.

My two sisters and I went to dig for potatoes with our hands. We had no tools. It was a beautiful autumn day. The birds were singing overhead. The air carried the scent of the harvest in the field. For a moment, I felt so free, thinking, "Oh, if only it would be so nice and quiet always! If only we could live in peace and not be hungry."

The silence was shattered by the rumble of a wagon. I looked up. As it came closer, I recognized the riders. It was the two Nazi hoodlums. I continued to talk nervously to my sisters, barely breathing. "The wagon has stopped! The two are getting out. They're taking aim with their guns!" I followed their line of sight. "They're aiming it at an older Jewish man. Oh no, it's our father!" I exclaimed in horror. My father was on his way to help us dig for potatoes.

God was with my father that time. A miracle happened: the rifles did not go off. Probably, they had used up all their ammunition the night before and had been too drunk to reload. My father quickly turned back and ran away. The beauty of the surroundings had now become dark and frightening. We went home; it was enough for one day.

Divine justice eventually caught up with these two Nazis. One day, they were found hanging from a pole in front of the Nazi army office. With time, they had angered the gentile peasants by subjecting them to the same cruelty. The Nazi army commander did not want civil unrest. He had the two deserters court-martialled and hung them publicly to pacify the angry local population. Their death gave us the false hope that in time justice might still prevail.

Nazi soldiers often used us for their amusement. Every day, new ideas occurred to them. It was winter, very cold, twenty to thirty degrees below zero and there was a snowstorm. Jews were ordered to clean the streets, the sidewalks, the roads, and even the highways with hand shovels — if they had any. Then they had another idea: we had to clean the snow off the roofs of the houses where they lived. Those of us who were younger wanted to spare the older ones this task. But the Nazis would have none of it. They had more fun watching old men climb up, slip on a steep, icy roof, fall down and break a leg, an arm or a couple of ribs.

Another amusement for the Nazis involved a young couple with six-month-old twin boys. One day, two Nazis walked into their house and took the twins into the backyard. One Nazi held the babies, tore out their arms and legs and threw them high into the air. The other Nazi aimed and shot at these limbs for target practice. They amused themselves, laughing, until both babies were torn to pieces.

Every day when I got up, the first thing I did was look out the window. If I saw anything wrong, I told my parents, who would go outside and find out what had happened during the night. One morning, I looked out in shock and terror. Lying just in front of our house were the bodies of two people, their hands and legs sticking up into the air. I started to shout. Everyone in the house rushed to join me at the window.

We later found out that this young couple had tried to resist arrest and were shot on the spot near our house. They didn't die immediately but twisted and writhed for some time in the sub-zero night. The quantities of blood they lost froze around them. Finally their limbs came to rest, frozen into the grotesque positions which I had seen. This young couple were the parents of the six-month-old twin babies who had been torn to pieces and had gone through so much misery already.

The transports to forced labour camps began in May 1942. A group of three hundred and fifty young men from our town was taken away to an *Arbeitslager*, a slave labour camp that was set up in the town of Gancevich.

Further transports to the labour camp were to follow. Gancevich was located in the heart of the Polesie region and was surrounded by swamps. Prior to the war, many Jews had made their living from that town's timberlands. Now Jews from Lenin and Pogost Zagorodski would be forced to perform hard labour working in the saw mills, building roads and unloading railway cars on the Baranovich-Luniniec line.

Because he was young and single, my brother Kopel was selected for this first transport. We all thought Kopel had less chance of surviving because he had never been physically strong and because he would refuse to eat any food which was not kosher. My father said that he would go in Kopel's place, but Kopel refused. "Father, do we know with any certainty that it is safer to remain here in town? Fate has called me to the labour camp; I will go."

The whole town was worried about Kopel. Several boys

Kopel's age volunteered to go to the train station in Mikashevich to replace him, but by the time they got there, the crammed train had already departed. Even the *Judenrat* became concerned and tried to bring Kopel home from the labour camp, though it was they who had initially assigned him to the transport. They wrote letters to the head of the Gestapo asking him to let Kopel go. They wrote that he was unwell and would not endure the conditions of the camp. The *Judenrat* still believed that the Nazis were amenable to reason and humanity. In 1941, no one was yet aware of the mass killings.

One day, the Jewish overseer in the Gancevich labour camp was notified that a grave had been dug and one of the Jewish labourers was to be shot. The next day, several Nazis came to see the head of the labour camp, asking for a Kopel "Lazebik" (rather than "Lazebnik"), who was ill and therefore not fit to work. The overseer realized that they intended to kill Kopel. They showed him the name on a list. Fortunately, the spelling of my brother's name happened to be wrong. The overseer said that there was no one by such name in the camp. Furthermore, he assured them, all workers were healthy and productive. The Nazis gave up and left. It was meant for Kopel to survive.

Chapter Five

GHETTO AND LIQUIDATION

ON MAY 10, 1942, the Nazis created a ghetto in Lenin. With no advance warning, they forced the Jewish population out of their own homes and into an old Jewish part of town in an area as small as two city blocks. Fifty to sixty people were crowded into each small house. Close to two thousand people were crammed into those few houses.

The ghetto was surrounded by barbed wire, with only one gate by which to enter. It was forbidden for Jews to leave the ghetto. Only those with special permits which allowed them to work outside the ghetto could venture out and then they had to be accompanied by soldiers to and from work. The ghetto was a prison from which there was no escape. The Nazis and their collaborators stood by the gate with machine guns, day and night. On the east side was the Sluch River. On the west side was the lake. To the north and south were swamps.

By this time, most Jewish males from approximately sixteen to fifty years of age had already been deported to the forced labour camp at Gancevich. Only women, children, the sick and elderly were left in the ghetto. Our numbers had been reduced from close to six thousand to less than two thousand. Some had escaped; others had been killed.

The Nazis imposed numerous restrictions on our lives in the ghetto. Those of us who were left were treated as sources of slave labour by the Nazis. We were afraid to be sick, because then we would be considered a burden to the Nazis and might be shot. We could not be too young nor too old, because then we could not work. It was forbidden even to give birth to a child.

People tried to find ways to adapt to these outrageous requirements. Some registered as younger. The young ones registered that they were older and tried to look older. Girls wore high heels. Boys soiled their faces to disguise their innocent young skin and wore the clothes of older people. The sick kept their pain to themselves.

Living conditions in the ghetto were abysmal. There was no food for days, no warm clothes for the cold and rampant illness such as typhus. Children's faces and bellies were distorted from hunger. Starvation and disease in the ghetto caused dozens of deaths each day. The Christian population in our town often tried to smuggle food to us into the ghetto, but this was a very dangerous activity, punishable by death. Those who took the risk were very brave.

From early morning to late at night, people congregated in the courtyards behind the little houses, sharing news, complaining and crying to each other and giving support whenever they could. Women worried about their husbands and brothers away in labour camps. Children played to forget their hunger and their fears. Everyone wondered how much longer the suffering would last. Would there ever be an end to this war?

Because my brother-in-law was a doctor, we were placed in a relatively good house in the ghetto, the last house on the street and the one closest to the river. My parents, my two sisters Esther and Sonia, my little brother Boruch, Esther's husband, Sonia's two children and I lived in this house with several other families, most of whom were strangers to us. At the time, Grainom was in Vilna and both Kopel and Moishe had been taken to the Gancevich forced labour camp. The house we were given was a well appointed house with beautiful old carved wooden furniture, but we would gladly have traded the furniture for a piece of bread. The owner of the house was an old Jewish man whose daughter Basia was a friend of Sonia. Before the ghetto was established, he and Basia lived in the house by themselves. Now the house was packed with people, one family per room.

I was one of the lucky ones who had a permit which allowed me to leave the ghetto in order to continue my work in the photo studio located in our old house. For the time being our house had remained unoccupied. The photo equipment and supplies were still there, as was the darkroom. All Jewish homes outside the ghetto were now left unlocked, under the nominal care of the *soltis*, the head of the gentile community. All the furniture and other precious belongings were slated by the Nazis for eventual shipment to Germany.

Having access to the world outside the ghetto, I might have taken the risk of escaping, but I was afraid my family would be harmed. Knowing the importance of close family ties in our community, the Nazis often took advantage of our vulnerability. Many strong, daring young people wanted to escape to the woods and join the partisan fighters, but they were afraid their families would be killed by the Nazis in retaliation. This posed many dilemmas. Should a son or daughter leave elderly parents and endanger their lives? Should a husband forsake his wife and children? Others felt that their responsibility was to remain with their community. Was it more morally right to leave the ghetto community and confront the enemy as a free agent or should one stay to protect the populace? Never before had we been confronted with moral issues of such magnitude.

During my visits to our old house, I often bartered with the farmers. The farmers needed shoes, dresses, coats, blouses and shirts and I managed to obtain these items in the ghetto to trade for food. Knowing I would be there, the farmers would come to my house with bread, potatoes and grains. During the summer, they also brought vegetables and whatever else they could smuggle past the Nazis.

I risked my life getting food for my family, and for others, too. One young Jewish woman who lived with us in the ghetto asked me to take an expensive suit to trade with the peasants. Even without the fur collar — trimmed off earlier for the Nazis — it was still a beautiful suit, made of very good fabric. I smuggled her suit past the guards out of the ghetto. Unfortunately, on that day, no farmers showed up to trade. Because I couldn't take the risk of returning the suit to the ghetto, I hid it in the attic of our house between the roof and ceiling walls, where I had hidden some other things that I couldn't sell.

When I returned to work the next morning, everything in the attic was gone. It had all been stolen by some townspeople. My heart fell. Naturally, I couldn't report the theft. No one from the gentile population could know that I was trading with the farmers. For a Jew, this would mean death if the Nazis found out. I felt especially bad for the woman who had given me her good suit to trade for food. She was not to get even a crust of bread for it.

One day as I worked in our house, my brother Boruch came by on the way from his work. He too worked outside the ghetto, at a dairy farm, and was part of a group of Jewish labourers that was led out of the ghetto daily. He looked very tired and I told him to rest for a while. I needed to wash the negatives I was developing at the moment and I asked him to keep an eye on the film while I went out for a pail of water.

When I came back, I found Boruch looking very pale and frightened. He was standing in the corner, tightly pressed against the wall. With guilt in his eyes, he told me in an almost inaudible voice that a group of local gentile boys had come into the house, grabbed one of the rolls of negatives that had already been hung to dry and run out with it.

I was terrified that I had lost the Nazis' film. I shouted at my brother, "Why did you let him take it? You know what the Nazis will do to me now? My life is finished. They will kill the whole family!" Later I was ashamed of myself for my outburst at my poor little twelve year old brother.

My brother started to cry. He had been afraid of the gentile boys and had not dared to oppose them or run after them. He knew that a Jewish boy did not have a chance in a fight with a group of gentiles. Besides, he had been brought up to be polite to people, not to fight.

Regaining my composure, I ran to the home of the *soltis*, the head of the gentile population appointed by the Nazis, and told him what had happened. I knew that, as a Jew, I was forbidden to enter the home of a gentile, but at the moment it didn't matter to me.

The *soltis* was himself scared, because he had been ordered by the Nazis to protect the Jewish homes against looting by the local population. He was responsible for the goods which the Nazis intended to ship to Germany. After some thought, he went to the home of some boys he suspected and, with help from their parents, found out that the boys had thrown the film into the lake.

The film was over a metre long and was found floating on top of the water. The *soltis* himself went out onto the lake in a boat and fished the film out. Relieved, I returned to the house, washed the film and hung it up to dry. Then I sat down and cried for a long time. The Nazis never found out about their temporary loss.

In this time of suffering and pain, there were times when we felt a resurgence of life, if only for a fleeting moment. One day, I took the liberty of bringing my sister's two year old daughter Leah to work with me. When we came into the house, Leah recognized it and joyfully ran out into the backyard. She began to dance and pretended to fly like a butterfly, singing, jumping and shouting. Her eyes lit up with excitement and freedom. Our congested old backyard was a delight for Leah, just as it had been for us as children.

As I watched her, I was overcome with emotion. My little niece, I thought, who knows how much longer you will be able to dance and be happy like this? What kind of a future is waiting for you? My throat was choking; I wanted to cry, but how could I, when she seemed so happy in her innocence? She was so young, innocent and beautiful. I had never felt the terror of deep uncertainty like this before. My own future seemed inconsequential compared to hers. Circumstances had forced me to look at life as an adult long before my time. When I finally took her back into the ghetto, Leah had forgotten her hunger.

⚓

It was five o'clock in the morning. The sky was dark, the clouds were low and about to fall in on us. The ghetto was wakened. For the first time, we were ordered to assemble — our first round-up by the Nazis. We thought that they were going to kill us, and that this was the end. We all knew that three long trenches had been dug several weeks before on a little hill on the outskirts of the town, near the hospital.

Before they were sent to the labour camp at Gancevich, some of our young able-bodied Jewish men had been forced to prepare these trenches. We knew the trenches had been dug for us and we felt helpless. As we stood together at the assembly square, the Nazis counted us several times, and then ordered us back to the ghetto. Those people who had stayed away from the assembly were later ferreted out by the Nazis and murdered.

Several days later, the *Gebiets-kommissar*, the top Nazi official of the area, arrived in town and everyone became frightened again. Why was this top Nazi official in Lenin? What was going to happen now? A Nazi soldier came to our house in the ghetto shouting for me to follow him to Gestapo headquarters where I was to take a portrait of the *Gebiets-kommissar*. When we arrived at the Gestapo office, the *Gebiets-kommissar* sat down on a chair in front of my camera and shouted, "It better be good, or else you'll be kaput!" I was too frightened to look at him, at the face of a wild animal, a man who was responsible for a multitude of deaths. Instead, I looked through the lens into the camera.

I took one picture, then became fearful that he would not like the cruel, bestial expression on his own face. I said to myself, "This is no good. He will kill me for sure." With a trembling voice, I asked him to smile for a second photo. I, a Jew, actually asked the *Gebiets-kommissar* to smile. And he did. With his threatening eyes, he still looked like a beast to me. I made two portraits and tinted them in natural colours. Luckily, he was satisfied with the portraits.

Heavy clouds hung over the ghetto. It was yet another morning, but it was still dark and most people were asleep. Suddenly, loud voices, then shouting: the second assembly. Everyone in the ghetto was driven out again. At the assembly square, children were crying, awakened and hungry. Again, we were counted, and then sent back to our houses. Fewer people hid this time. We all remembered the fate of the first evaders. Once again, those who had not appeared to be counted were tracked down and shot.

⚶

At dusk on August 13, 1942, the ghetto was quiet. Another day of hunger, beatings and hard labour was coming to a close. In our house, nobody was asleep yet. Again I was called to take my camera and go to Gestapo headquarters. It had become almost routine for me to be ordered to go to the *Ortkommandature* to take pictures. This time, however, it was different. When I arrived, I was told to leave the camera and go home.

Now I was worried. I wondered why they would make me leave the camera. Without it, I would not be needed any more. The camera was my life. For a picture, I could occasionally get a piece of bread. What would I do now? I cried all the way back to the ghetto.

When I came home, my family looked at me. "What happened? Why are you crying?" my mother asked. I answered, "They took my camera away."

My mother put her hand on my shoulder and tried to comfort me. "Why are you crying over a camera?" she implored. "Look at all we've lost. We've lost our house, our clothes, jewellery, fur coats, gold, silver and our freedom. The camera is nothing by comparison."

A few hours later, another Nazi officer walked in. I knew him; he had brought me several black-and-white portraits of his family to tint, a job which I had not yet completed. He asked me to return his pictures to him immediately; he had changed his mind. He knew very well his true reason for retrieving the photographs, but he didn't say a word. He just took his pictures and left.

From these events, I had a premonition of the tragedy that was about to occur. Again and again I repeated, "They took my camera. The officer took his wife's pictures. What does this mean?" No one else in my family realized the ominous significance of these events. The Nazis knew that the next morning was to be our last. This is why the camera and the pictures were taken back from me. If my parents had only paid more attention to what I was saying, might they have had time to hide or escape?

That night, I was so worried I couldn't sleep. I was still a child, but maturity had been thrust upon me by our circumstances. Having taken on adult responsibilities early in life, I felt responsible for my whole family. After a long time, I finally dozed off.

At dawn, we were awakened: "Out! Out! Another assembly. All out!" Half-asleep, I jumped up and looked around. Everybody in the house had already gone, except for my sister Sonia and her two children. She desperately wanted her children to be dressed in clean clothes. Perhaps she somehow knew what was to come. I could not leave her alone — she might be killed if she were found in the house — so I helped her dress the children: clean underwear, a clean shirt, clean pants, a clean little dress for Leah. The children were very quiet and allowed themselves to be dressed very quickly. It seemed that they too knew what was happening. One could see it in their forlorn eyes. I could not say anything to them. Instead, I embraced them, feeling their tender young bodies against me. I hugged them without a word.

When I came to the assembly square, I knew this time it was different. Someone yelled to me, "Walk straight ahead to the Germans." To this day, I don't know whose voice it was.

Sonia's two children, Borchke and Leah.

But like an automaton, I went where I was told. I wound up right in front of the *Gebiets-kommissar* whose portraits I had taken several weeks before. He recognized me right away and called me over, away from the rest of the crowd.

I begged him, "Let me have my little brother." I wanted desperately to have Boruch with me in the last hour of our lives. But the *Gebiets-kommissar* did not listen to me. With his animal face, he nodded to an SS soldier standing beside him. The soldier butted me with the end of his rifle and shouted, "Walk!"

I didn't know where I was being led. Was I going to be shot? I walked as though I were hypnotized. No way to describe the terror of the moment. I continued walking, as the soldier pointed his rifle at me from behind. How much longer, how many more minutes or seconds of life were left for me? I waited for the bullet.

Suddenly the soldier ordered me to turn in the direction of the synagogue, away from the killing ground. Hope flickered through my mind. Would I be spared? Would I be the only survivor out of nearly two thousand? The Nazi soldier ordered me to enter the synagogue and left.

I walked into the synagogue to find a group of Jews in the sanctuary, also singled out from the rest of the population. My delay as I had helped my sister with her children had caused me to miss the selection. Now I realized that, when everybody had assembled this time, the Nazis had gathered a few craftspeople whose talents they might need. Picked were those with small families — less people to keep alive. A tailor with six or seven children was far less desirable than one with two or three children.

Altogether, they spared five Jewish families from the town of Lenin: those of a carpenter, a shoemaker, a tailor, a blacksmith and a painter. There were twenty-six people in all. I was the twenty-seventh and the last one. I had become valuable to the Nazis as a photographer and processor of photographs. In their obsessive need to record their evil acts, my life had been spared. Because I had been a last-minute choice, I was also the only one without my family.

I knew these were the last minutes of my family's life. I felt I was drowning in an ocean of pain and sorrow. I didn't want to be left by myself. What was the point of being the only survivor of my family? I wanted to run out and die with the rest of my family. The others in the synagogue held me inside against my wishes. They said if I ran out, they would all be killed.

I climbed up to the attic of the synagogue and through a small window watched open trucks being loaded with people and then being driven to the three trenches. Others walked in small groups towards the trenches, with rifles pointed at their backs. Among them, I found out later, were my sister Sonia and her two children. On the way, she had begged the gentile

August 14, 1942. The trench in Lenin.

people they passed to save her children. Nobody offered to take them in. I was also told that at the trenches, the waiting Nazis and their Lithuanian accomplices forced many to undress completely, even the children and the elderly.

I heard the Nazis open fire with their machine-guns. The trenches were far away, but I heard the cries of my people, cries that still echo in my ears. I am still filled with indescribable sorrow when I think of how they came to their end. I flinch even today whenever I hear the roar of a crowd at an outdoor sports arena, sounds that reverberate.

The massacre of the Jews in the nearby town of Mikashevich.

All were killed and buried in those three long trenches, including my father, my mother, my little brother Boruch and both my sisters Sonia and Esther, Esther's husband, as well as Sonia's two children, two and four years of age. My mother and father were barely in their fifties when they were executed by the Nazis. Sonia was shot and her two children were buried alive in one of the trenches, as was my little brother Boruch. The Nazis did not waste bullets on children. Moishe's wife and young son, who had moved back to Lenin at the beginning of the war, were also killed. The Nazis had offered to spare Esther's husband's life because of his abilities as a doctor. But when he asked that they spare Esther's life as well, they refused. He joined Esther in the trenches.

One thousand eight hundred and fifty Jewish people were executed at the orders of the *Gebiets-kommissar*, assisted by SS men, their Lithuanian collaborators and the local police from our town. The Nazis took pictures of the killing. They later gave me the films to develop and I made copies for myself. Was this why my life had been spared?

When the shooting was over, I climbed down from the attic and walked to the ark where the Torahs were kept. I sat down in front of this familiar symbol of my people. I didn't cry; I was frozen with shock. I couldn't move any part of my body. I just stared at the curtain behind which the Torahs were kept. Oh, God, will it ever be possible for me to avenge these acts? God, where are You? Good people, where are you? Where is justice?

⋘

I didn't move away from the ark until hours later when a few SS men brought us back to the ghetto, which was still under guard. They put us all into one large house with five rooms, each family to a room. For me, there was no room. I slept on the floor in the hall.

The next morning, I was allowed to leave the house and walk around in the ghetto. I immediately went to the house where my family had lived and the room where I had helped Sonia dress the children just the day before. It was dead quiet. All the rooms were empty. Just yesterday, this house was overflowing with people, hungry, depressed, worried — but still alive. Now they were all dead. I burst into tears. Here I could cry. Nobody could see me now.

The bare walls of the room stared at me. The floor was littered with the discarded clothes of my sister's two children, dropped on the floor in our rush to leave. Now I started to pick up the clothing. I folded each article of clothing neatly, hugging and kissing each little item. I carefully put the clothes in a drawer, one piece at a time. I knew that the children would never again wear them. But somehow I felt that by folding their clothing, I was comforting the children, hugging them. This gave me momentary comfort.

When I closed my eyes, I imagined my mother blessing the candles on a Friday night and all the family around me. I longed for my family, for my former life. A lump stuck in my throat. I thought again of the senseless brutality and inhuman cruelty that had resulted in the end of my world. I leaned my face against the cold bare walls and wept bitterly.

I walked out of the house into the courtyard, which had been full of people. The events of the previous day had always been discussed here: how many had been killed in the last few days, how many had died of hunger, and how many were still struggling to keep their lives. Now the courtyard was empty. I walked across to the barn. Its door was open and I walked in.

Suddenly, I heard a noise from the rafters in the barn. I lifted up my head, and saw two big eyes shining from above. Then I saw a face. It was Basia, my sister Sonia's girlfriend, in whose house we had lived. She had been hiding in the hay since the final round-up. She whispered to me, "Is Esther alive?" I answered, "No, she is dead. Everybody is dead." Basia asked, "What shall I do?" I replied, "Hide, and then, if you can, run away as soon as possible." I left the barn. I was afraid that I would be endangering her if someone heard us talking.

I walked out of the house through the silent, lifeless ghetto. It seemed like a cemetery with each house a gravestone. Some doors were open; some were closed. From time to time,

I heard a cry: cats looking for food. There was no one left to open the doors for them.

All the inmates of our house were slowly put back to work. The men were sent out to labour; the women were ordered to do domestic work for the Nazis. I was summoned to report to the Gestapo headquarters again. But now I was totally apathetic. Nothing mattered to me. I felt depressed and full of grief.

Before the war, farmers from the neighbouring villages had come to church on Sundays and brought their produce to trade with the Jews. This activity stopped when we were confined to the ghetto. The farmers would have had to pass through the ghetto, which was not permitted, in order to reach the church. This Sunday, they came again, aware that there was no longer a ghetto nor a Jewish population in Lenin. Instead of going to church, hundreds of gentile farmers from the vicinity stood around the small bridge bordering the ghetto.

To get to the Gestapo headquarters, I had to cross this bridge. I will never forget the moment when I had to face the gentile farmers. I felt humiliated and heavy with loss; all my people were dead. How could I look into the faces of those gentiles gathered on the bridge?

Slowly and deliberately, I started to walk, my heart pounding. As I approached the bridge, I saw the people staring in my direction. I forced my head up in defiance. They could not look me in the eyes either as I crossed the bridge. To my relief, all heads turned away from me. Perhaps they were afraid of meeting the ghosts of those people who had been their neighbours, their friends. Perhaps they were ashamed of those others who called themselves Christians. I drifted across the bridge and was gone.

❦

*The Soviet monument to those massacred August 14, 1942
in Lenin; that the victims were Jews is not mentioned.*

Today the only marker of life in Lenin is a monument which
the Soviets erected after the war at the site of the three
trenches. It reads: "Here lie 1,850 Russian citizens murdered
by the fascists." It does not state that those murdered were
Jews. Every year on the anniversary of the murders, flowers
are placed on the graves.

Chapter Six

JOINING THE PARTISANS

*A*T THE GESTAPO headquarters, the Nazis treated me as though nothing had happened. They gave back my camera and assigned a Ukrainian girl named Marisha as an assistant to me. They instructed me to teach her my trade. It was obvious that she was going to replace me and that I would soon become redundant to them.

For almost two weeks, I worked with Marisha in the darkroom. I resisted by teaching her as little as possible. But she was persistent. She wanted to know more and more. I taught her never to open undeveloped film or photographic paper in even the faintest light. This allowed me to pack away all the photographs of my family in the darkroom; she thought that they were undeveloped materials and took good care of them.

Back in the ghetto in the midst of yet another uncomfortable night in the drafty hall, I woke up in a panic, thinking, "What will happen to me? The Ukrainian girl will soon learn my trade and I will be killed. There is nothing for me here but death. I must escape." But if I escaped, I would endanger the lives of twenty-six others.

Two weeks had passed since my family had been murdered. I lived in this house with five families, the sole Jewish survivors of Lenin, but I felt totally isolated. The five families had each other. And I was left alone in the world. Outside the house, I was surrounded by enemies. I tossed and turned, contemplating my terrible dilemma.

Suddenly I heard shooting outside, sirens wailing. Everyone in the house woke up and looked out the windows. People were running in the streets: Nazis, collaborators and partisans. We knew the Soviet partisans had attacked Lenin.

What should we do now, run or stay? I wanted to run and join the partisans. The others said, "No! You want to run because you are alone. We have families. It is too dangerous for us." The shooting was now becoming more intense.

There was a sharp knock on the door. In the doorway stood a partisan, a tall, young Jewish boy from our town, dressed half in military and half in civilian clothes, with a gun and several grenades hanging on his belt. In his hand was an automatic rifle. He said to us, "We heard about you. I came to tell you to escape. Save yourselves! Run as fast as you can! We have killed many of the murderers. If you stay, tomorrow all of you will be tortured and shot."

Now, the group decided to escape. With bullets still flying in the air, I ran with all my strength in the direction of the forest, out of the ghetto and out of town. Dead bodies lay everywhere. When I reached the outskirts of our town, a couple of partisans stopped me. "Where are you running?" they asked. I answered, "I'm running away from the ghetto. I want to join the partisans. Let me come with you!"

They replied, "Not so fast. First, you must have permission from the commander." It was difficult for an unarmed Jew to be accepted by the partisans — especially a woman. They pointed me in the direction they had last seen the commander. I ran on, asking every partisan I met, "Where do I find the commander?" By the time I found him, I was shaking with fear. He was dressed in a Soviet military uniform, with guns on both sides of his belt and an automatic rifle. He asked my name. When I told him my name, he knew who I was. He knew that the Nazis had kept me alive to work for them as a photographer. He also knew that my sister was married to Dr. Feldman, and that both had been killed. He then presumed that since my brother-in-law had been a doctor I would know how to look after the wounded. "You will come with us," he ordered.

The fighting had ended. The partisans were returning to their bases, and I was with them and alive. It felt like a dream. I had been accepted into the Soviet partisans! I wasn't sure what was waiting for me now, what kind of a life I would have. But I knew I was very lucky. I was now a partisan, no longer afraid of the Nazis. I tore off the yellow star of David. We started our journey into the woods.

⚓︎

After a couple of hours walking on the rough bumpy grounds to the woods, I was exhausted. My shoes were not suitable for the rough path and swamps and soon fell apart. At times, I sank in mud up to my knees.

The severely wounded were transported on a wagon. Crammed with wounded partisans, the wooden wagon shook along on the rough ground behind the single horse that dragged it. I can imagine how much pain the wounded must have been suffering. The horse was small and scrawny. He, too, was exhausted.

I overheard one partisan saying to another, "The horse is perspiring. He has to be covered up. Otherwise he won't make it much farther. But there are no blankets." If the horse collapsed we would have to carry the wounded on our shoulders to the next village where we might get a fresh horse. I was the only one with a coat. Without hesitation, I took off my coat and gave it to cover the horse.

After another couple of hours, we were still on the move. We paused only for very short rests, because it was too dangerous to linger. The enemy was close. For the partisans who had left their base yesterday, it was the second day of walking. By now, I was barely dragging myself along. I was not used to walking such long distances and I was thin and undernourished. My shoes were gone. I walked barefoot and my feet were scraped and bleeding. Though I could speak Russian perfectly, I was afraid to ask how much longer we had to walk. I was now part of the Soviet partisans and I knew that in the Soviet Union one didn't ask too many questions. I knew I was being watched to determine my fitness.

Suddenly a young, blond partisan handed me a beautiful pair of boots. "These are for you. Wear them," he said. I understood that they had belonged to a Nazi soldier. With a sense of irony and tears in my eyes, I put them on. They were too big, but my feet were swollen and at least with boots my feet would be covered. I couldn't pay him for the boots. Money did not exist among the partisans and I certainly didn't have any. I think he gave me the boots as a gesture of appreciation for my having given them my coat to cover the horse.

The sun was setting. When we arrived at the partisan base, it was already dark. Only the moon gave us some light. As I stood beside the wagon exhausted, a tall young woman named Tania introduced herself to me in Russian. She said she was a nurse and I would be working with her.

Tania explained, "There are many wounded people here and there is a lot of work to do. But right now you must rest. You must be very tired."

I asked her quietly, "Where do I go to sleep?" We were in

the middle of the woods with no buildings of any kind near-by. She answered quickly, "You sleep on what you are stand-ing. The forest is big. Find yourself a place, any place. Then lie down and go to sleep."

I lay down under a tall, old tree. Its protruding roots pressed against the bones of my forty kilogram body. I could not fall asleep. I realized that from now on my bed would be the grass, my roof the sky and my walls the trees. I tried to cover myself with my coat, which they had returned to me. It was soaked through with sweat from the horse. The stink was almost unbearable.

Was I tough enough to withstand these living conditions? Would I be strong enough to keep up with the partisans on a mission? Most were trained to fight and used to living under these conditions. I closed my eyes and prayed, "Oh God! Give me the strength and the courage to confront all this, and give me life and health to be able to do my work."

I was grateful to be alive and realized how lucky I was to be among the partisans, away from the murdering Nazis. I knew that many Jewish girls would be happy to be in my place. The circle of my life had turned. No more slavery, no more eyes looking down on me, no more threats. Though my life was still in danger, I felt human again. Physical and emo-tional pain loomed, as did hunger, suffering and the primi-tiveness of our existence. But I was alive. I would have to learn to adapt.

A gun was in my hand now. I would learn to shoot, to aim at the enemy. Now, if the enemy pointed his gun on me, I could shoot back. I had the opportunity to avenge the blood of my mother, my father, my sisters, my brother and my sister's two children. I was not afraid of being killed. Responsible only for myself, I no longer had much to lose except for my life. I was prepared to do everything in my power to help the partisans in their fight against our common enemy. I was proud to join the ranks of freedom fighters who lived and fought in occupied territory.

I also felt strength in knowing I was one of thousands of Jewish youth among the partisans. They were Jews from cities and farms, Jews from towns and villages, young men and women raised in a tradition of learning and culture to respect one another. They were a peace-loving people who had known nothing of war. Few had ever handled a rifle; now they were forced to fight for their lives. Torn from the lives they had once known, they stood up and fought like lions. Young Jewish partisans were known as the most daring of all.

I remember before the war, when a Polish officer would come to our house and put his rifle in the corner of the room, I would keep as far away from it as possible. My parents had taught me that a rifle meant danger. But now a rifle was a friend. It meant survival, vengeance and self defence.

I had never dreamt that I would be thinking like this. I never expected to be holding a rifle, and not only to hold one, but to learn how to take one apart and clean it daily. I learned all this and more so that the rifle lying beside me on the wet ground would work when I needed it. A rifle among the partisans was a passport; it was also my pillow. As long the war continued, I would never part with it. I resolved to volunteer for active combat operations, to fight for my people — for Jewish dignity and Jewish honour — and for an end to the Nazi killing machine.

~

I was a partisan from September 1942 to July 1944 when we were liberated by the Soviet army. We were guerrilla fighters who fought mostly in small scale ground combat operations,

A partisan detachment in White Russia.

dangerous but highly effective in harassing the enemy. We destroyed railroad tracks, blew up enemy trains filled with munitions and food heading for the front line. We destroyed highways, set up ambushes, attacked towns and villages occupied by the Nazis. We demolished bridges and fortifications, disrupting communications and supply lines to the enemy troops. We engaged in counter-propaganda and tried to win support from the local population. Our goal was to hinder the enemy in any way we could.

My brigade was the Molotava Brigade. It was said our brigade had the best and most disciplined fighters in the province of Minsk. It was mostly made up of experienced Soviet officers and soldiers who had escaped from Nazi prison camps. Others were soldiers who had remained in the swamps of Polesie and the surrounding villages when the Soviet army had retreated in the summer of 1941. They had remained in occupied territory in order to practise guerrilla warfare against

the Nazis. Our brigade, headed by Misha Gerasimov, consisted of more than two thousand people. Under our brigade were nine detachments. Few members were identifiable Jews. Those who were Jewish kept it to themselves. When I joined, we were eight women; two of us were nurses.

Our base was located in the forests of Polesie between Pinsk and Lenin. The area came to host five brigades, under the command of Vasily Zakharovich Komarov (Korzh) and Alexei Yefimovich Kleschov. Komarov, a veteran of the Russian civil war who had been born in Pinsk, was among the first to organize partisan groups in the area of Lyuban, Lenino Zhitokovichi, Starobino and Pinsk. Kleschov was first secretary of the Communist Party in the province of Pinsk. The Komarov/Kleschov *Sodjenie*, as we were called, was a force to be reckoned with. Farther to the west, around Brest-Litovsk, functioned another group of brigades, commanded by Sergei Ivanovich. We had effective communication with each other as well as with Moscow.

During the Second World War, the Soviet Union had the largest partisan organization which included the largest number of Jewish partisans. It is estimated that there were approximately 200,000 in the Soviet partisan movement at its peak, and approximately 20,000 to 25,000 were Jews. In relation to the Jewish population, this was an inordinately large percentage. In what was once called White Russia, Jewish partisans were at the forefront of propaganda, resistance and sabotage against the Nazis.

Faced with death in the ghetto or deportation to a concentration camp, many Jews fled to the woods and marshlands for safety. Some were intent on joining the partisans. Many Jewish boys and girls were rejected by the partisans because they were Jewish and they had no firearms. Physical strength and military experience were the most important prerequisites for being accepted by the partisans. If either of these criteria were lacking, then the possession of a weapon was sufficient. But obtaining a weapon was not easy. Gentiles were often reluctant to sell guns to a Jew. Often Jews had to resort to illegal purchase, robbery or acquisition in battle to find arms. Using improvised fake rifles for intimidation, they sometimes managed to fool peasants into supplying them with guns and pistols.

A Jew arriving in the forest had to face a series of new tribulations: adaptation to life in the woods, the hunt for weapons, hostility from those partisans who were anti-Semitic, continuous wandering in search of food. There was also the constant danger of exposure while unarmed, critical when the surrounding areas were populated by hostile peasants and villagers. There was a lack of trust and communication between Jews and the surrounding communities. Some of this was due to anti-Semitism and some to outright fear of Nazi retaliation for collaborating with their enemies — Jews, partisans, communists. Too often local inhabitants were quick to betray Jews.

Those who were too young, too ill or too old to fight went into hiding in the forest and set up civilian camps. Some civilians worked for the partisans as tailors, shoemakers, welders, bakers, barbers and other essential tradesmen.

Jewish partisans were committed to supporting these civilian camps. They protected them and often brought food and clothing. They saw it as their duty to save as many Jewish lives as possible, even if a large number of civilians in the woods increased the danger of discovery. It was often a serious point of contention between Jewish and gentile partisans whether to offer help and protection to these Jewish refugees.

In the woods, Jewish partisans found themselves fighting a multitude of Nazi-sponsored local bandit groups who were

particularly anti-Semitic and always on the lookout for Jews. There were various bandit groups: Acovces, Bulbovces, Bandarovces and Vlasovces, to name a few. The Vlasovces, for example, were soldiers of the Russian liberation army organized by the Nazis and under the command of Lieutenant-General Andrei Vlasov. A general in the Soviet Army, Vlasov had been taken prisoner by the Germans in the summer of 1942. He had persuaded them to establish an "army" recruited from among Soviet prisoners of war. This "army" was organized to fight on the side of the Nazis, overthrow the communist regime in the Soviet Union, and establish a pro-Nazi Russian state. Vlasov's army was used for operations against the partisans and took part in anti-Jewish actions. Most of the bandit groups were fighting each other and all of them killed Jewish people.

Hundreds of Jews were killed by our own Soviet partisans. In 1941 the partisan movement was struggling. Spies, traitors and Nazi collaborators among the populace abounded. Many partisans were ambushed and killed. In frustration, the commander of the Pinsk partisan units issued an order to kill every stranger in the woods who was not attached to a partisan group.

Unaffiliated strangers were immediately shot. Most were Jews who had escaped from ghettos or camps and were hiding in the woods. They did not belong to any combat unit because the partisans did not want them. How cruel that those lucky enough to have escaped from the Nazis into the forest survived only to be shot as spies. Hundreds were killed before the commander realized his error; he was targeting innocent Jews and not Nazi spies. By the time he called off the order, it was too late for too many.

The persecution Jews endured wherever they turned — in the ghettos, in the concentration camps, in the hard labour camps, hiding in the woods — continued even within the partisan movement. All partisans, Jew and gentile alike, faced the same basic risks on dangerous assignments. But the Jew, in addition, faced unresolvable complications. Jews had to prove themselves in battle by volunteering for the most dangerous missions. Among the partisans as among the Nazis, the Jew was subjected to collective responsibility. One Jewish partisan's failure was the failure of all Jews, but his or her triumphs went to the credit of the detachment and its commander.

Jewish partisans found themselves under constant scrutiny and in a constant struggle to justify their right to fight. If a Jew was brave and walked at the head of the line to be first to attack, the anti-Semites would say, "Hey! Why are you in front of us? Are you better than we are? You are running ahead of us!" If the Jewish fighter kept in the rear, they said,

Harmony in death. Jewish and gentile partisans buried in one grave; 1943.

"Hey! Why are you lagging behind? You must be a coward!"
There was nothing worse among the partisans than to be
labelled a coward.

In spite of the problems with anti-Semitism within the
partisan organization, Jewish partisans fought heroically.
They often became leaders in the woods: Jews were at the
head of approximately two hundred bands of partisans. Jews
participated in many of the underground Soviet organizations, though often not openly as Jews. Jewish partisans also
died in far greater numbers than their gentile counterparts.

Chapter Seven

PARTISAN NURSE, SOLDIER AND PHOTOGRAPHER

I WAS APPOINTED AS A nurse in our partisan unit of the Molotava Brigade. With no medical training, it was not an easy job. Though I had initially been accepted into the partisans because they knew my brother-in-law had been a doctor and assumed that I had medical skills, in fact, I had no medical training or experience.

My first challenge was to overcome my fear and squeamishness about blood and open wounds. Before I could learn what I needed to know on the job, I had to get used to dealing with injured, ill and dying people. I tried to imagine myself lying alone on the ground, riddled with bullets. Would I not want someone to care for me, to bandage my bleeding wounds? Only through such images could I find the strength to overcome my fears and learn to care for the wounded.

I received hands-on training from the principal doctor in our brigade, Ivan Vasilievich. Originally from Eastern Russia, he had been a major in the Soviet army and was trained as a veterinarian. He came to his position as doctor because of the shortage of doctors among the partisans. Few gentile doctors were prepared to leave their families and take part in the difficult and dangerous life of the partisans. It was much more safe and comfortable to practise in the towns and cities. For Jewish doctors, there was of course greater motivation for joining the partisans. It was a way of escaping the Nazis. But too many Jewish doctors, like my brother-in-law, had already been killed by the Nazis. Therefore it was not surprising that our main doctor was a veterinarian; at least he had been trained in medicine.

Sometimes, Ivan Vasilievich's veterinary training came in handy. One morning the cook asked me what to prepare for the wounded. I pointed to a lamb hanging skinned and washed on a tree. The cook looked at it and refused; the lamb was covered with worms. When I told Ivan, his face brightened. He said with a smile, "I am going to examine that meat. You know that I am a veterinarian. I know more about animals than I do about people." He examined the hanging lamb and hurried back to the cook. "Don't worry, you can cook it. This type of worm only infests fresh meat." The problem was solved. The cook brushed off the worms and proceeded to make the wounded partisans a good meal.

Ivan was very kind and patient with me and became my mentor and friend. I reminded him of his daughter, who was about my age. He appreciated my reliability and felt that he could depend on me. At every opportunity, Ivan taught me everything he could about medicine, giving me intensive medical training on how to treat and deal with all kinds of casualties.

Ivan also taught me many things about survival — about how to act and what to say in order to be accepted by the partisans. He was one of the few Soviet officers who were not anti-Semitic. This advice, and Ivan himself, was on many occasions to save my life.

Ivan Vasilievich held a position of prestige in our brigade,

Faye tending a wounded partisan during a raid.

often attending executive meetings at brigade headquarters. He knew all the officers and their official secrets: what was going on, who was to be commended, who was on the hit list.

There was a time when I myself was targeted on that hit list. There was a false rumour that I had gold jewellery that I was withholding from the commander — and hence from the Soviet government. During those difficult war years, people killed for a gold watch, ring, a bracelet, a chain or anything else made of gold. I knew it was much safer without gold. Ivan supported me, telling the executive, "She has distinguished herself by making personal sacrifices and by helping our comrade partisans in the face of danger." He himself would take responsibility for me, guaranteeing that I had no gold. Somehow Ivan managed to persuade the executive of my integrity. I am still grateful to Ivan for his help, devotion and friendship — and for his unique contribution in teaching me how to heal people.

With Ivan's help, I soon found myself able to care for partisans wounded in every part of the body, by every type of bullet, shrapnel and shell. A wound caused by a bullet that passed cleanly through the body and out again was not too bad. But when the bullet lodged in the body, the situation was much more serious and we would have to operate. The most difficult circumstance was when an exploding bullet hit the body, tearing out parts of the flesh. Medication was very limited in the woods. Salt water was the only available disinfectant for the wounded. We therefore could never spare salt for cooking. Vodka was the main anaesthetic.

There was always a drastic shortage of bandages. With so many critically wounded partisans, I often had to use sheets torn into long strips for bandages. When they got soiled, I washed them clean, sterilizing them in a pail of boiling water over the campfire. They had to be used over and over again. Unfortunately, not even sheets were always available. All this was not bad when the weather was mild and dry. Winter, when it was freezing cold, or rainy summer days posed other problems.

Most difficult of all was when we had to move the wounded to safer places during an attack by the Nazis. We had to move the wounded very quickly and methodically, always at short notice. People were assigned to help the wounded; sometimes we had horse-drawn wagons. I was often in charge of the whole procedure, since I was best acquainted with the capabilities of the wounded.

Since Ivan rotated among several detachments, I was often left by myself with the wounded with no doctor present. In emergencies, I dug out bullets, sewed together skin, cleansed infections and changed dressings. I even became a surgeon. All operations were done in the open air, with an "operating table" made of branches cut from trees.

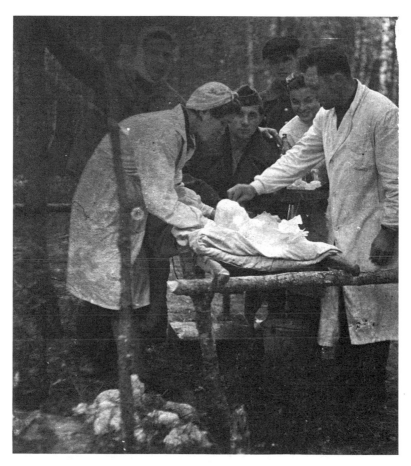

Faye assisting at an operation. She had already tended the partisan with the bandaged face in the background.

Once, I remember, there was a partisan, Pavel, in command of a detachment, who had been shot in the finger. All the flesh and skin from his finger was gone, with just the bone sticking out. When the wound would not heal, I had to use my common sense. I thought that if I cut off the bone, the flesh and skin would later heal, and this was what I did. While my patient lay on the grass, I gave him lots of vodka until he became drunk to the point of unconsciousness. Then

I took a pair of pliers which I had sterilized in boiling water and started to cut the bone off. It wasn't working satisfactorily. Halfway through, I removed the pliers and broke off the bone with my teeth. Pavel did not make a sound, but cold sweat ran down his face. The operation was successful. Pavel recuperated quickly and his wound healed.

Sometimes my work was more tedious than difficult. Another partisan had been shot in his neck. The bullet had exploded, tearing out all the flesh under his chin and leaving a hole in his neck. His teeth and lower jaw had been dislocated. The poor man lay on the grass in agony unable to move, his bandages soaked in blood. The smell of blood attracted flies to him like a magnet, and I sat beside him chasing away the persistent flies. I could not stop fanning him even for one second. It was difficult to sit waving my hand above his face for hours on end. For days I sat with him, day and night, keeping the flies away, trying to keep up his morale. From time to time, I fed my patient egg yolks, drop by drop, to give him strength. Often the food didn't go down his throat when he swallowed, but ran out through the hole in his neck.

My colleagues, seeing how tired I was, offered to help and would relieve me for short periods of time. Nurses inspired a special sense of respect amongst the partisans. My colleagues also felt sorry for me, though I didn't complain. I knew that, though my work was hard, my discomfort could not be compared with my patient's agony. Once, he had even gestured for me to give him a gun; he wanted to kill himself. When he got stronger, Ivan Vasilievich was able to operate on him with Tania's and my assistance. It was a complicated operation. The lower jaw was moved back into place and kept aligned with wire. My patient recovered and became a brave partisan once again.

Given my lack of experience, not to mention the recent

horrors I had been through, assisting at an operation or changing the dressing on a wounded partisan was an enormous strain on my nerves. Under such emotional strain, my mind would begin to wander and I would lose track of reality. Suddenly, I would see strange, horrible images before my eyes: my father bleeding to death or my mother shot through the neck. The blood of the operations in which I took part would become the blood of my sisters and brothers twisting in torture. Had they been shot in the same parts of the body? Had they also bled so much? I would shut my eyes for a while, sending my mind back to the three trenches where my family had been killed. Which members of my family had died first? Did my sister see my mother shot or did my mother have to watch my twelve year old brother die? The youngest brother, whom I loved so much, would in one more year have had his bar mitzvah. All this would go through my mind, and more, much more.

A cry of pain from the patient would bring me back to reality. I was now in the present; there was a wounded partisan who needed my help. Back to the practical realities of partisan life, I continued to mind the wounded. Thank goodness there was little time for reveries. My work kept me preoccupied.

In that autumn of 1942, my first among the partisans, I was looking after another severely wounded partisan. The "doctor" in charge at the time — I believe he was just a medical student before the war — pointed to him and said, "This partisan should be washed." I answered, "Comrade Doctor, how can I wash him? He has a fever. It is cold and windy and there is no shelter." It was late in the fall; the leaves had fallen off the trees days ago. "Never mind, wash him." That was an order. There was nothing more to say. I had to obey my superior.

As I washed my patient, he began to shake. His temperature soared. That whole night he was burning hot and delirious. In the morning, he quieted down. As I put the thermometer under his arm, he said to me, "I appreciate and thank you for all you have done for me. I know how much you care. I will never forget you." Ten minutes later, I came back to remove the thermometer. He was dead.

I became frightened and ran off to tell the doctor. I never went back to the dead boy because I couldn't bear to face him. He was buried with the thermometer under his arm. I had neglected to take it out and was left without a thermometer.

✼

Along with my responsibilities as a nurse, I was also a partisan soldier, always ready for combat duty. When I heard that the partisans were going to raid Lenin again, I immediately volunteered. While in Lenin, I hoped to retrieve my camera and all my photo supplies and thus to be able to resume my work as a photographer. I would chronicle the activities of the partisans. Just as important to me, if not more so, was the chance to find my family pictures, which I had hidden in one of the boxes of undeveloped photo supplies at my house.

We left our base at sunset. After long hours of walking in the night, we reached the outskirts of town and divided into small groups. Each group had a strategic Nazi-occupied house to attack. It was still dark. We moved in, making sure that we were not noticed. Then the order came to attack: a gun shot, a loud voice calling, "Fire!" Our guns thundered into the shattered silence of the night. There were explosions, a cacophony of sound waves, firing weapons mixed with the shouting of hundreds of partisans. The enemy responded with confused fire.

Faye at rifle practice; early 1943.

After an eternal hour, the shooting died down as the enemy went into temporary retreat. This was the short period of time when we could collect the supplies we needed. Now I rushed to my old house for my photo supplies; they were gone. I surmised that Marisha, my assistant, had "inherited" all my possessions. Determined, I asked two of my partisan friends to accompany me to her parents' house. There my uneasiness turned to relief. There was no need to enter Marisha's house; her mother had put all the photo supplies, including my camera, on the front sidewalk. She must have guessed that when the partisans attacked the town, I might return for them. Though Marisha's mother was prepared to help me reclaim my possessions, Marisha herself had escaped with the Nazis — another collaborator.

I was grateful to retrieve my family pictures, my camera, and my photo supplies. Among these were the chemicals needed to make my own developer. At that time there was no such thing as ready-made developer. I knew by heart the formula for my own developer — all six ingredients, their quantity and sequence. The developer ingredients were engraved in my mind. My life had depended on it.

While I gathered my supplies together in front of the house, a woman who I did not know came by. She handed me the leopard-skin coat the Nazis had taken from me. Though I didn't know her, she obviously knew who I was. I had bought this coat when Lenin was still under Soviet rule. A shipment of leopard-skin coats had been brought in from Russia. Though at the time recovery of the coat seemed so much less important than my recovery of the photo supplies, later in the winter in the forest it was this coat that kept me warm. It was so light, so warm and so strong.

When we returned to our base, my problem was to figure out how to keep my photo equipment safely in the woods. We were constantly on the move, sent from one assignment to another. Just as frequently, our headquarters would be attacked and we would have to scatter in small groups in different directions and find new places to set up camp. When the enemy cleared out, we would eventually return to our base, which was the meeting point for joining the rest of our brigade.

It would be impossible to carry all of my equipment along with me wherever I went. My rifle, gun and grenade were heavy enough as it was. Along with these, I also carried my medical bag filled with all my supplies, the clean bandages and salt water to be used as disinfectant for the wounded. The only solution was to leave all my photographic equipment buried in the ground whenever we had to change location for a short time. The equipment was kept underground in one of the bunkers at headquarters the rest of the time.

I always received help with my equipment from my fellow partisans. They wanted me to be able to take photographs during lulls in the fighting. In fact I was ordered to take photos. My own commander, Misha, once threatened me, "This better be a good picture; otherwise you will be sorry." Sometimes I was expected to be in the photo myself. I would prepare the camera, adjust the focus and ask someone else to press the button.

Over the course of my two years with the partisans, I took over a hundred photographs. I developed the photographs under the most primitive of conditions. There was no darkroom or photo laboratory, but I managed with the help of blankets to develop the film on the ground. Lying on the grass in the summer or on the snow in the winter was not easy, but I had been practising photography since I was a child and always found a way to make do. All I needed was a quiet moment in a shady place far from everyone where I would not be disturbed.

<hr />

Partisan raids on Lenin took place frequently. Another group was getting ready to attack Nazi headquarters in my town. Again I volunteered to go with them. I had retrieved my photographic supplies, but with so many wounded partisans, I desperately needed more medical supplies.

After the usual surprise attack and temporary retreat of the Nazis, I ran into one of the houses that the enemies had just left. A quick look around and my eyes fastened on a carton of beautiful white bandages. I was delighted and quickly took the box, thinking I would have bandages for a long time. But unfortunately when I returned to our base I found out that the bandages were for casts. Soft when wet, they dried to the hardness of a rock. The plaster in them had to be washed away before I could use them.

When we returned to our base, I realized that washing out the plaster would not be an easy task. I needed water. The river was half an hour's walk from our base, and not a very safe walk. I went for water and started to wash the bandages. As I vigorously scrubbed the bandages, the skin from the palms of my hands rubbed off and the flesh became exposed. When I finished my task, my hands were sore, but I didn't pay much attention to this. It was time to change the dressings for the wounded partisans. The bandages were clean, but my hand became inflamed.

One night a few days later I found I couldn't sleep. My hand was throbbing badly and my whole arm was swollen. I knew that I had a fever. My forehead was hot and I was shivering. Evidently the pus from the wounded partisans whom I was attending got into the open flesh on my palm and infected my whole arm. Rubber gloves did not exist. I was in terrible pain and frantic. What was going to happen now? Should I tell the authorities in the morning that I was sick? This was not a good idea. It was too risky. I remembered a few weeks earlier one of the Jewish partisans had a painfully sore finger. He felt he couldn't pull the trigger on his rifle and refused to go on an assignment. Because the authorities didn't believe he was badly injured and felt he was shirking his responsibility, he was shot.

Frightened, I feared I would now become fatally ill without anyone knowing. I had helped so many ill people. Now I needed to help myself. I got up from the wet grass where I lay and walked back and forth, looking up to the sky for comfort. There was a full moon throwing light between the long shadows of the tall trees. I went to fetch my first aid kit and took out a sharp knife which I washed several times with alcohol. In the moonlight, I could see where the inflamed sore had to be opened. My lips were closed tight, but my eyes were wide open. I lanced the pocket of pus. As it splashed out, my knees collapsed. I had to lie down, but I wouldn't cry. Shortly thereafter, I fell asleep and slept all night. In the morning, I felt much better. The pain, the fever and the swelling were gone. Wounds healed very quickly in the woods.

I was always more tired than the others. Usually when we were at the end of a mission and stopped for a rest, everyone else went to sleep except for the guards and I. This was the time when I tended to the wounded, changed their dressings and fed them.

Once on a mission I was so tired that I feel asleep as I was walking and bumped into a wooden post. I had hurt myself, but had to disregard the pain since I needed to catch up with the rest of the group. A couple of days passed before I had a chance to wash off the mud in which I was covered. When my hand was clean, I was able to see a splinter so big I almost passed out at the sight of it. I had to remove it. I took a pair of tweezers from my first aid kit, washed them in alcohol and pulled out the splinter. After all these years, there is still a blue mark on my hand from the black tar with which the post had been painted and which had spread into the flesh of my hand. Now I realize how tired I must have been not to have felt any pain whatsoever when I bumped into that post.

I never told anyone about these personal mishaps. I was all alone and had only myself to rely on. A mere nineteen-year-old, I continued to make these life-and-death decisions on my own. I felt so lonely, so abandoned. Sometimes I did not care what happened to me, but most of the time I remembered that I was perhaps the sole survivor from my family. It was only through me that their memory would live on. Only this thought gave me the strength to continue.

Chapter Eight

MY BROTHERS AS PARTISANS

*I*N FACT I was not the sole survivor from my family. On August 14, 1942 — the same day the ghetto liquidation in Lenin had taken place — the labourers in Gancevich returned from work to be told by a Nazi officer what had happened in their hometown. In shock, they heard that the entire Jewish community — their mothers, fathers, brothers, sisters, wives and children — had all been murdered.

At Gancevich, the inmates had been forced to perform hard labour under the worst possible conditions. They were hungry, dirty, covered with lice and crowded forty or fifty to a room. Many had thought about escaping into the woods and joining the partisans. But they had been warned that, if just one labourer were missing, their families back in the ghetto would be killed. Despite the inhumane conditions, they were not prepared to risk the lives of their families. Now there was nothing to keep them in Gancevich, nothing more to lose. Most of the three hundred men immediately escaped to the woods. They headed east towards partisan territory, oblivious to the shooting at their backs. Among them were my two older brothers, Moishe and Kopel.

The Nazis immediately started a chase and search operation. The twenty workers who had been out working at the time of the escape and had remained behind were killed as scapegoats by the Nazis.

It was getting late in the day, and the woods grew dark. The escapees paused to get their bearings. They organized themselves into smaller groups. That way, they could spread out and be less noticeable. Their goal was to reach and join the partisan units.

Among them was a respected man named Dvorin who wanted to organize a group. Before the war, Dvorin had been a wealthy and influential business man. He was sharp, capable and had much life experience. Through his business travels, he had become very familiar with the surrounding countryside. His business connections had made him respected and valued by the farmers and peasants in the area.

Dvorin asked my brother Kopel to join. At first Kopel was flattered that Dvorin had chosen him. Then he remembered that he had had a dream a few days earlier in which he had been warned to avoid Dvorin. It was strange, but somehow he remembered this dream and decided not to go with Dvorin's group. Instead Kopel escaped together with my older brother Moishe. The dream proved prescient. Dvorin's group were later captured and hanged.

Among the escapees were five brothers who had been our neighbours in Lenin. They were a very close family and had stayed together during the escape from Gancevich. Their group was also captured the same day. The Nazis forced each brother to hang the other, one by one. Many others were captured that day, but the majority managed to escape. My two brothers were among the survivors.

Like all Jews who escaped to the forest, their lives were constantly in danger. My brothers had to cope with an extremely hostile environment without food, warm clothing or guns. They had no guns and Moishe had no military experience. They lived through six weeks of struggle and rejection by various partisan groups until finally they were accepted into different partisan units. They had to separate because it was easier to be accepted as an individual.

I had heard about the escape from Gancevich and was desperate to find out if my brothers were still alive somewhere among the partisans. I was especially concerned about Kopel because of his ill health and because he was religious. Religious belief was scarcely a credential for the Soviet partisans. In November 1942, I found out that a group of partisans in my unit were about to go on a mission. I asked Tania, who was to join them, to enquire after my brothers wherever she went. We knew it was like looking for a needle in a haystack, but she promised to do this for me.

When Tania returned, she had good news. She had asked every partisan they passed about my brothers. At last they had come to a partisan group called the Voroshilava Brigade — on guard was my brother Kopel! She told him that I was alive and in her brigade. Tania returned with a note from Kopel confirming that he was alive and in good health.

I was so grateful that Kopel was alive. I was desperate to see him, talk with him, and tell him what had happened to our family, how they had been killed, to share with him the details of what the Nazis had perpetrated on the whole town. I wanted us to grieve together. I couldn't keep it to myself any longer; I needed to share our tragedy.

I didn't have to wait long. Another group was going east on a mission and this time they let me come along. Before I left I asked my commander if he would accept my brother into our brigade. He said, "If your brother is as good a worker and as brave a partisan as you are, bring him along." I was happy and grateful. Our mission included a stop thirty kilometres from my brother's base where we were to blow up a small bridge. When we completed our task, I went to look for my brother.

I could have gone by myself, since his base was nearby. I had a rifle, a gun and I always carried a grenade on my belt with which to blow myself up if I were to be captured alive. Jewish partisans were routinely hanged in public after interrogation under torture. For this reason no Jewish partisans allowed themselves to fall into Nazi hands alive. Better to kill oneself with a hand grenade.

As a Jew and a woman, I had to be extra cautious — even with my own partisans. Just travelling on my own would give the anti-Semites in our group the opportunity to accuse me of being a spy. To avoid suspicion, I asked a colleague to accompany me. Our departure was scheduled for dawn.

As I was getting ready for sleep, another partisan pulled me aside. He whispered that my companion-to-be planned to murder me in the woods. I was terribly agitated. Again I was faced with a life-and-death decision. As far as I knew, my companion was trustworthy. My instincts told me to have confidence in him. I knew him as well as I knew his accuser. Perhaps the accuser was lying. If I didn't go with him in the morning, I wouldn't be able to see my brother. And, if he did indeed intend to kill me, well, I too had a rifle.

I made up my mind to go with him. We left at dawn. On our way my eyes were always on his hands. I watched his every move. Could it be true that he wanted to kill me? Or had the other partisan played a cruel joke on me? It was a long walk through the forest because we had to take alternative routes that we knew would be safe. By the time we came to my brother's detachment, it was almost dark. And I knew that it had been a cruel joke or deception: I was safe with my companion.

When I came face to face with Kopel, we couldn't believe our joy. We were both alive and together again. I was no longer alone. Our eyes filled with tears of gratitude, and we fell into each others' arms.

A Jewish civilian camp. Kopel (third left) assisted
the families by bringing them food; 1943

I asked my brother's commander if he would allow Kopel
to join my detachment, so we could stay together. I told him
that my commander had given his permission. "Tell your
commander that I would not exchange ten Russian partisans
for this one Jewish boy," he said. "I will not let him go." My

brother said to me, "Let it be this way. It may be safer to separate. Maybe one of us will survive."

Before the war, my brother had been a devout rabbi. But it was his former military service for the Polish army which stood him in good stead now. Kopel was an expert rifleman, and always volunteered for attacks and other dangerous operations. He was often the first to be sent as a messenger and the first in battle. The others in his detachment gave him much deserved respect. He not only went when ordered, but also volunteered to take the place of others on scouting missions. Being totally observant of *kashrut*, the kosher food laws, he used these missions to get milk, cheese, butter, yogurt and other foods he could eat. It was extraordinary, but during his whole time among the partisans, Kopel managed to keep kosher.

Most important to him was to give support to the Jewish families living in the civilian camps in the forest whose situation was so precarious. Kopel helped them by bringing food and clothing and protecting them whenever he could. He was not strong or tall, but he was completely fearless, often risking his life without concern for himself.

We sat down together and I began to tell Kopel about the ghetto and the killings. Before we could complete this longed-for reunion, before we could find solace in each other, we were interrupted by a sudden alarm. The Nazis were attacking. Kopel looked at me. "Who knows if we will have a chance to meet again. Goodbye, good luck and may God be with you. Have courage. Be strong and take a strong stand in these difficult times." With these words, we parted.

Kopel ran one way to take his position in the dugouts and to defend against the enemy, and I with my partisan friend went in the other direction, back to our own group. I prayed my brother would survive the Nazi attack.

Chapter Nine

RAIKA

*T*HE PARTISANS continued their raids on Lenin, hoping the Nazis would abandon it. But it was of strategic importance and the Nazis continued to return. Despite the emotional cost, I participated in these raids, first to retrieve my precious photographs and photographic supplies and later to obtain much needed medical supplies. In my final return to Lenin, I would come to burn down my own home. But in the interim, I participated in raids whenever it was necessary.

After one such raid in Lenin, our unit had reassembled ready to depart. Suddenly the wife of the priest, whom I knew vaguely from before the Nazi occupation, came running up to me. She was hiding a Jewish girl, eight years of age. Just before the ghetto had been liquidated, the little girl had appeared at her door with a letter written by her mother, begging the priest's wife to save her daughter. The priest's wife took her in, but was afraid to keep her any longer. Her husband was the Greek Orthodox priest who had taken over from the elderly priest for whom the whole town had celebrated his fiftieth anniversary. Her husband had already been taken to Siberia and people were becoming suspicious because she was buying more food than she needed for herself. It was too dangerous. She said she was afraid that if the Nazis found out she was hiding a Jew, they would kill the child and her too. Knowing I was Jewish, she entreated me to take the little girl.

I felt it was my duty to save a Jewish child, but I needed permission from the commander. When I made my request, the commander became angry. "You know that we cannot accept children among the partisans! She won't survive. And she will endanger the rest of us." I knew the truth of what he was saying, but in all good conscience I could not keep myself from helping a Jewish child. I had only to think of my little brother, of my niece and nephew. I was prepared to endure hardships, to endanger my own life by assuming full responsibility for this child.

I pleaded with the commander, saying that I would take care of her just as I took care of the wounded partisans. She would be my responsibility. I would watch over her and look after her. My courage and persistence must have persuaded him; eventually he agreed.

I was happy to be able to save a human life. In truth, I saved two human lives. Aware that she had been seen with the Jewish girl, the priest's wife immediately left town for another city. Her escape was successful.

A month later, in December 1942, all the gentile White Russian inhabitants of Lenin, about five thousand in number, were assembled and herded into a large barracks. The priest's wife, had she not fled, would have been among them. The Nazis surrounded the building with heavy artillery and set it on fire. Anyone attempting to escape was immediately shot. This was the end of Lenin.

After the final murder of its populace, all of Lenin's buildings were torched to the ground. Those who had escaped and returned after the war found the site unrecognizable, covered in weeds. They couldn't find the streets or the houses — just emptiness, dead silence and graves. Except for the weeds, all

Faye and Raika (centre) with a group of wounded partisans.

life in Lenin had ceased to exist. There was no trace left of
our beautiful town and the fine people who had lived there.

At the time, I was unaware of Lenin's fate and conscious
only of the challenge that faced me. The girl's name was
Raika Kliger. From then on she was with me all the time. I
took care of her, except when I was sent on various missions
and Raika remained at our base. It was not easy to include a
young child among the partisans. She caused a lot of trouble.
Raika was a willful child and my expectations of her were
very high. I was not ready for the role of mother. Sometimes
it was more obligation than love that kept me linked to her.
But if I had the choice, I would do it again.

While I tended the wounded, Raika would play in the
woods near me. She amused herself, as any child of her age
would, by running around and playing pretend games.
Sometimes she would carelessly run beyond the guard lines,
which was forbidden. And for good reason. Wherever a
partisan base was established, guards were always stationed to

look out for Nazi ambushes. If they saw interlopers, the
guards would raise the alarm and we would run to take our
defensive positions. It was therefore forbidden to go outside
the guard lines. But an eight-year-old didn't understand the
rules or the danger.

Many partisans were suspicious of Raika. They concluded
that she was a spy. Some even called her "Spy" rather than by
her name. And they presumed with ridiculous logic that if
Raika were a spy, I was also a spy. "Logic" also dictated that
we should therefore both be shot.

I did have friends among the partisans who supported me.
I had risked my life so many times to fight the enemy and to
help the wounded; surely my loyalty was obvious to those who
were prepared to see it. Again it was my mentor, the doctor
Ivan Vasilievich, who came to my aid. When he heard the
speculation that others wanted to kill Raika and me, he went
to the commander of our brigade to vouch for us, swearing
that we were not spies. Once again they believed him. The
taint of treachery was lifted, at least for the moment.

Nothing was easy with Raika to care for. Once we were
travelling through dangerous territory to change our base.
Raika had been with me for many months. We passed by
some farmers' houses; we had been plodding wearily through
the woods and needed to stop for a rest. It was a scorching
summer day. We knew the Nazis were close by and were not
allowed to enter any of the houses.

When we were ready to move on, I noticed that Raika was
missing. I asked if anybody had seen her; no one had. We
could not continue to our destination without her. The partisans cared nothing about Raika's well-being. They did fear that
she might fall into enemy hands and tell the Nazis vital information about us — how many were in our group, in which
direction we were heading. Such information would make it

possible for the Nazis to surround, attack and kill us all.

It was noon. Raika was still missing. The sun was high and it was very hot. Everybody was drenched in sweat and we were all tired and thirsty. It was dangerous to remain in the area for so long. The commander was very angry. Of course we all knew that Raika was my responsibility. I was frantic; I searched everywhere for my charge.

When we were almost ready to give up, Raika appeared. I noticed her from far away, as she ran towards us. She was very frightened, thinking she had lost us, and ran very quickly from quite a distance. As she reached us, she fell unconscious to the ground, shaking with convulsions. Her face was very red. I didn't know what to do. Ivan calmed me down, saying she was only overheated. He told me to let her lie quietly on the ground. She would come to in no time and be fine. Worried, I waited impatiently.

When she finally opened her eyes, I asked her where she had been. She answered innocently, "I went into a house to get some milk." I told her, "You knew you were not supposed to go anywhere. You must stay with the group. You could have been killed and you put the whole group in danger. All this for a little milk. Never do that again!" She promised, but there was always a first time for another type of mischief.

Not all our trials were because of Raika's childish disobedience, however. One day, as I was busy minding the wounded, Raika was playing a few hundred feet away from me. Suddenly she started to run towards me, shouting. She fell into my arms weeping, pointing in the direction of another partisan. The partisan's rifle was aimed at where Raika had been playing. I knew this young man. He had learned that Raika possessed a watch that her mother had given her for her birthday. For this man, a watch was worth killing a child for. He clearly had been intending to shoot her.

I took the watch from Raika's wrist and threw it in the bushes. The poor child began to cry. How could she give up that watch, her only memento from her mother? But I didn't give in. I knew that it was safer for her without a watch. It was for her own good, for her very survival. She, of course, couldn't understand this and her childish heart remained inconsolable for a long time.

Once I was forced to be separated from Raika for seven days while I was with a group of partisans on a special mission. It was too dangerous to take Raika with me, so she was left at our base. In the meantime, the remainder of our unit had to move the base to a safer placer. They took Raika with them, but there was nobody to take particular care of her. Raika was placed on a wagon with wounded partisans and some older girls who did much of the domestic work in the campground.

It was a cold autumn. One of the older girls took Raika's coat, leaving her shivering from the cold. Nobody paid any attention to her; nobody cared. When I returned after seven days, I hardly recognized Raika. She had lost weight; her face looked very pale. But what frightened me most of all was that she was covered with lice.

Cleanliness was one of my highest priorities, to avoid catching typhus fever, which was epidemic among the partisans. Typhus is transmitted by lice. Every day, when I boiled the bandages to sterilize and re-use them, I also boiled my underwear and all my clothes. That way I could be assured of keeping clean. Though I was constantly around the sick, I never caught typhus. Raika used to sleep beside me, but now I could not let her close to me.

Everything Raika was wearing was dotted with lice. Her hair was full of them — in the thousands. Even her eyebrows were covered with lice. I washed her clean. There was no choice but to cut off her beautiful blond curly hair. I took off all her clothes and threw them into the campfire. In a short time, she was back to normal again. Thank goodness, she never caught typhus.

I boiled my belongings in secret. No one else could afford such a luxury. I thought that no one saw me, that no one paid attention to what I was doing. But the following incident showed that I was mistaken. It was at dawn. I was still asleep. A messenger came running to me and woke me up, "You are ordered to go to the headquarters immediately! At alarm speed! Quickly!" I worried about what the emergency could be. As usual, I had taken off my clothes for the night in order to wash them and was wearing only underwear. This way I would have clean dry clothes for the next day. I slept covered with my sheepskin jacket. Not having time to get dressed, I put my three-quarter length sheepskin jacket on over my underwear, buckled up my belt with gun and grenade and ran with my rifle to headquarters.

Looking as though I were fully dressed, I stood at attention before the brigade commander. After examining me from head to toe, he said, "You are being tested. A partisan should always be ready for enemy attack. I was told that you were sleeping undressed. Clearly it isn't true. You can go back now." Going to sleep undressed was against partisan regulations. I took a deep breath, turned around and disappeared back into the woods. I realized I must be even more careful. There were eyes watching me all the time.

⚬⚬⚬

One winter day a handful of partisans from another brigade visited our detachment for a week. With this group was a Jewish doctor by the name of Blumovich. He brought us good news from the main partisan headquarters. An airplane was due to land on a secured strip out of enemy range and fly all our wounded partisans to safety in Moscow. This was a first for us. I was very happy.

In the meantime, I wanted to make sure that Dr. Blumovich was treated well. I served him the better meals, the same as the wounded were getting. He was very pleased with my courtesies. We became good friends. We talked, and he told me many stories of how Jews had distinguished themselves in battle against the enemy, and of how many had lost their lives. By this time Jews were more adequately armed and were more confident that the civilian camps in the woods would not be molested.

One of Dr. Blumovich's stories was about another Jewish nurse who had worked with him. She also participated in all major partisan operations, and was fearless as a railway saboteur. Once this young woman had been with a group on the way to blow up a section of the Brest-Pinsk railway track. The group ran into an enemy ambush. The situation was extreme and they decided to retreat. It was the young Jewish girl who had the courage to yell, "Cowards! Where are you running? Go! Forward!" Thus prodded, the partisans rushed at the enemy. The Nazis broke up and fled. Sadly, this courageous young woman was killed in a later battle.

When Dr. Blumovich left, we said goodbye to each other: next year in Jerusalem. We must each have been wondering if we would survive the year, much less the war. Dr. Blumovich did survive the war. When he was liberated he went to Israel where he changed his name to Atzmon. Later he became in charge of all medical services for the Israeli army, where he served during the Six-Day War. I did meet him in Israel, where I was his guest and was able to reminisce with him about the old times among the partisans.

Meanwhile, I was appointed to go with the group of

wounded partisans who were to be evacuated to Moscow. We were to be accompanied by well-armed partisans to guard us at the location where we were to meet the plane.

I realized this was a rare opportunity for Raika. I asked the commander for permission to take Raika with me. She too could be evacuated to the safety of Moscow. Though, after more than a year together, I was reluctant to see her go, I knew that the partisans barely tolerated her presence. This was a good chance to secure her safety. The commander agreed, saying it would be easier for all of us if she left, that it would be a good way to get rid of her.

It was December of 1943, an early winter, very cold. We dragged ourselves along in what seemed an endless trek, though it must have been only about thirty kilometres. The distance was not far, but it took us close to three weeks. We could not travel along a highway or even a regular road, but had to travel on circuitous routes. Day and night merged into one.

We had several combat encounters with the enemy along the way. When it was safe to stop and rest for a while, as usual it was in a secluded swamp. But it really did not matter: one place could be muddy and a few feet away we would find a comfortable frozen dry spot. We did not care — mud, water, swamps, dirt, ice — it was all the same to us as long as we could fall down on the ground to rest or sleep for a while. While we were moving, the scouts in front of us let us know if the roads were safe or if the enemy was close by.

We finally arrived safely at the appointed place to wait for the airplane. We waited a couple of weeks and still there was no sign of a plane. In the meantime, I had found out that Raika had an uncle in one of the partisan groups nearby. I notified him to come. He was very happy to know that Raika was alive, that there was at least one member of the family who had not been killed. I asked him to take Raika with him, since the plane to Moscow seemed a chimera. The uncle said he couldn't take her; his base was in too dangerous an area. I understood and assured him I would look after her. Then he left.

By now six weeks had passed. Some of the wounded had already recovered. I was ordered back to our base which had experienced more action and incurred more casualties. I was needed there. It was difficult for me to leave Raika alone. But this was an order and had to be obeyed. I kissed Raika good-bye, wished her good luck and left.

The plane still did not come. After I left, Raika decided to search out her uncle all by herself. Alone, she walked thirty kilometres through the woods. She came to her uncle's base only to find out that he had just been killed. He was eighteen years of age. There was nothing to do except go back. Several weeks later, the plane finally did arrive. The group of wounded, and Raika among them, were flown safely to Moscow. Raika would survive the war in Moscow. I never saw her or heard from her again.

Chapter Ten

PARTISAN FRIENDS AND FOES

WE ALL BELONGED to one brigade. We learned to live together, eat together, fight together and survive together. We also needed to get along with each other. Sometimes it was hard to live through one day, let alone years. There was a strong friendship, cooperation and loyalty amongst most of us and a willingness to help each other. In the forest, connections were made between disparate people. Cold, hunger, stress forced strangers to become like family. We were also comrades in arms, all dealing with the same life-and-death circumstances. Our lives were bonded by the dangerous conditions under which we constantly lived. A special bond, nonetheless, existed among those of us who had experienced similar horrors under the Nazis.

Jean was my best female friend among the partisans. She was a Jewish woman who came from a background similar to mine. We did not see each other often, because though she was in the same brigade, she was in a different detachment and was often away on combat missions. But the knowledge that she was there gave me a great deal of comfort.

Jean had been born in Drogichin, a town near Pinsk, and she was the only survivor in her family. In her town, the Nazis had killed the Jewish population using the same cruel method as in our town. They were shot in front of long trenches, then the bodies were covered with dirt. In Jean's town, however, before the Nazis could cover the trenches they were warned of a partisan attack. They ran off, leaving the trenches open and unguarded. Some of the victims were wounded but alive. Many who were wounded might have survived, but they did not have the strength to pull themselves out from underneath the dead bodies which covered them.

Jean had been shot through the throat. After some time, she regained consciousness, though in her shock, it took some time to convince herself that she was still alive, unlike the bodies surrounding her. She managed to climb out of the trenches. Naked, because the Nazis had stripped their victims before shooting them, she staggered to the nearby peasants' homes. She knocked at doors. Nobody would let her in. Doors were slammed and locked in her face.

She became so desperate that she went back to the trenches. She couldn't think of anything else to do. In despair, she lay down on top of the dead, waiting to die. Time passed. At last she realized that, though she had lost a lot of blood, she was not dying. Jean became afraid that in the impending daylight, the Nazis would come back. All the bodies, living and dead, would then be covered with dirt. Some around her were still crying weakly for help. Jean tried in vain to pull the wounded out from under the corpses, but she herself was too weak from loss of blood.

Again she dragged herself out of the trenches. Some old rags were hanging on a farmer's fence and Jean managed to wrap herself in them. She stumbled in the direction of the forest. She was near death when a group of partisans from our battalion found her a few weeks later.

The partisans brought her to me, since I was in charge of the wounded. Jean was nursed back to health, until she was

Faye with three other Jewish partisans.

ready to join the fighters. She told me, "My life came to an end when my family was murdered. I survived by a miracle. Every additional day of my life is not mine — it belongs to my family. I must avenge them."

Jean remained in my brigade. She became an excellent fighter, fearless and brave, an example for other partisans. She was one of the many women fighters who volunteered and made major contributions to our defence. Though women numbered only about two or three percent of a total unit in the Soviet partisan movement, they were essential as scouts and intelligence agents. Women were often less suspected of espionage than their male counterparts. Many women who volunteered for the partisans had training as nurses or radio operators and a large portion of partisan doctors were women. Sometimes women were assigned to combat missions alongside men on a continuous basis. These were the heroines of the partisans, and Jean was one of them. She went out on mission after dangerous mission, fought the enemy and managed to stay alive. Today, though she lives far from me, we still keep in touch and remember our shared partisan experiences.

Life among the partisans was a constant test of character. Jean's personality, her courage and fortitude, made it easy for me to feel a special link with her. Personality could also be a negative factor. Under the extreme conditions in which we lived, the personal qualities of the members of our unit took on serious consequences.

Sergei considered himself to be more important than anybody else, because he and the commander of the brigade were among the first to escape a Nazi prison camp and to organize a group of partisans. They had started the group with eight people and it had grown to a brigade of three thousand. When Sergei was wounded in the leg and unable to walk, he felt his needs demanded priority. The best food available to the wounded should, he felt, be given to him. Most of the time he had his way.

Tania was serving lunch to the wounded on a day when we had managed to get a few eggs. To the partisans, eggs were a delicacy. It was not often we had them. She served the eggs to another partisan more seriously wounded than Sergei. Sergei was enraged and began to shout and swear. The partisans often enhanced the Russian language with profanities. I guess it helped them to relieve the unrelenting tension.

But Sergei didn't stop with swearing. He took out his gun and, to Tania's astonishment, fired it at her. Luckily he didn't hit her, missing by inches. Men like Sergei were prepared to kill for a few eggs.

Grisha was Sergei's best friend. Grisha had escaped with Sergei from the Nazi prison camp and was also one of the eight partisans who had founded the detachment. Grisha was the opposite of Sergei in character, a modest, quiet boy. Grisha had also been wounded in the leg, but recovered quickly. Unlike Sergei, Grisha never wanted anything special for himself.

I didn't know Grisha well, but somehow I felt safe near him. Whenever we were together in a group, I always tried to stay close to Grisha. Inexplicably, this made Grisha uncomfortable. He would always say, "Why are you here? Can't you find another place to sit? Do you always have to be beside me?" I felt disheartened at these comments and couldn't understand why Grisha was always so careful to avoid me. The other young men enjoyed my company, often asking me to join them, to sit with them and talk.

Forty years later I found out the reason for this apparent aversion. My friend Jean told me that Grisha was Jewish. Nobody knew this; he had hidden his identity, afraid to admit that he was Jewish. Grisha felt it was much safer to be known as a Russian boy, especially with Sergei as his best friend. That was why he didn't want me near him, so no one would suspect he had something in common with me, a Jewish girl.

I understood Grisha's motivations because I myself many times pretended I was a Russian girl when I was among partisans who were unaware that I was Jewish. Since the partisans themselves were far from immune to anti-Semitism, it was so much easier and safer. I spoke Russian fluently, without an accent, so no one suspected.

Once I was ordered to take strategic photographs of specific places and people the leaders wanted to document. My commander sent two partisans to accompany me as guards and helpers. We went on horseback. It so happened that these partisans didn't know I was Jewish. When we were in the woods a long way from our base, a Jewish girl dressed in rags passed by. I felt sorry for this thin, pale, frightened young woman who looked exhausted and undernourished. She was probably hiding in the woods with her family because the partisans did not want to accept her. I was sure there must be a civilian camp nearby where more Jews were hiding.

One of my assistants said, "Oh, look! A Jewish girl. Oh! How I hate her! I hate all Jews. I would kill all of them." To me he turned and said, "My feelings towards you are different. You are Russian. It is a pleasure to be with you, to talk to you." Yes, he had a different view of me because he thought that I was Russian. My feelings towards him changed also. He was supposed to be my guard. What help could I expect from him if he found out who I really was? I kept silent and didn't reply. When I arrived at our destination, he probably found out who I was. I never saw him again.

Despite the kinship we felt in our common struggle, anti-Semitism continued to create tensions among us. About four months earlier, a group of partisans had blown up a train going west to Germany. It was winter. In the cattle cars they discovered two hundred cows that the Nazis had confiscated. The group returned to our base with all the cattle. The partisans in command soon realized the cows had to be cared for and milked. The commander ordered all the women in the brigade, Jews and gentiles alike, to milk the cows. Though we knew this was designated as woman's work, we were all willing

The partisan on the right had expressed to Faye his dislike of Jews,
not knowing at the time that Faye herself was Jewish.

to do it. We knew it was important to make ourselves indispensable to the partisans. I was excited also because I had actually had experience in milking a cow. When I was twelve years old my mother had become sick and wasn't well enough to milk our cow. I had taken her place. My father, who had looked on, had approved of my work.

For three days everything was fine. Then a rumour began that the Jewish girls didn't know how to milk cows properly and should be excluded. I was upset; the accusation simply was not true. I was sure that I did this work as well as the Russian girls and furthermore we had cooperated well together.

The accusations frightened me. Our position as women and Jews was always tenuous. Any sign that Jewish girls were not useful to the partisans put our lives in danger. If we were not needed, we could be expelled from the partisans. Such pressure was enough to make me lose confidence in myself.

In great frustration and anxiety, I began to cry.

My friend Ivan Vasilievich saw me and asked why I was crying. I told him, "I know how to milk a cow very well, and they rejected me. I am worried now." Laughing, he tried to convince me that they wouldn't throw me out of the partisans. "Don't worry, you do a hundred other things, things that none of the others can do. You are needed here. And furthermore, you should be happy that they would not let you milk the cows." He quieted me down and I got past my fears. I understood that this was just another anti-Semitic gesture.

Although it was sometimes explicit and sometimes unstated, the pressure was always there. Because I was Jewish, I had to work twice as hard to be deemed as worthy as the gentile girls. When I worked night and day I was told, "You are not like a Jewish girl. You are just like the Russian girls." This was meant to be a compliment. My response was always, "Yes, but I am Jewish." My work as a nurse, a photographer and most of all as a soldier was plentiful reason for me to stand tall, to be proud of myself and my heritage.

A while later, reconnaissance notified us that the Nazis were preparing a blockade. We had to find a safer place. Now what would we do with the cows? We couldn't take them with us, and we didn't want to leave them for the enemy. We had to leave the base quickly and not be noticed. We decided to kill the cows, and to bury them in the ground. It was winter; the meat would stay fresh, frozen for a long time. So the digging started as a few hundred partisans went to work. In one day everything was done. The meat was buried and we were all ready to abandon the base for the time being until the blockade was lifted.

Unfortunately, the blockade took much longer than we expected. It was five weeks later that we were finally able to return to our base. Meanwhile the snow had melted. All the meat that we buried in the ground had spoiled completely. We were terribly disappointed. The endless search for food would have to begin again. We were all hungry; during the blockade we hardly had a chance for a decent meal. There was not enough bread or water, let alone any meat. Such was our life; we had no choice but to adjust to it.

～

Although it was nature that had caused our disappointment with the precious store of meat, human nature could prove itself even more treacherous. One night, I woke up terrified by a premonition that something horrible was going to happen. I couldn't get back to sleep. Minutes later I saw a drunken officer barely able to stand weaving towards me. He could hardly stand up. The moon was shining; I could see clearly his red face and bloodshot eyes. As he stood over me, he mumbled, "This Jew, she doesn't like Russian boys. She wants a Jew. She doesn't like me. I will finish her off." He reached for his gun. I knew this officer, and could have predicted that something like this would happen. Drunk most of the time, this man was always after me and I always tried to avoid him. He thought that he could do whatever he wanted with a Jewish girl. Once he had tried to embrace me, but I managed to run away. At the time, he had told me, "I will get you sometime."

I was sitting on the ground pressed tightly against the tree under which I had been sleeping. The officer squeezed the trigger but nothing happened. This is why.

He and a group of other officers had been up all night at headquarters drinking vodka. After many drinks, he got up and loudly proclaimed, "I have to go now. I'm going to shoot her." My luck held only because my friend Ivan Vasilievich once again came to the rescue. Although he did not drink, Ivan had been with the drinking party. When the drunkard made his proclamation, Ivan surreptitiously took his gun from him, unloaded it and handed it back. The officer was so drunk he didn't even notice. Lurching from side to side, he began to head towards the area in the forest where I slept. Ivan and two others followed and managed to drag the drunken officer away from me, but only after the first shot had been fired.

If I wanted to stay alive, I would have to keep away from such men. I knew the rules regarding sexual conduct in our brigade very well. In our brigade, sex was forbidden. I am not sure about the rules in other partisan groups, but in ours sex was punishable by death. There were those young men who in secret went to look for women in the villages, thoughtless of the risks they were taking. We were surrounded by enemies and traitors. The Nazis knew our boys were seeking out girls in nearby villages, so they exploited this situation by injecting many of the young girls with venereal diseases. As a result, many young men caught sexually transmitted diseases and became very sick.

Mostly, however, sex was not a major issue in our group. We didn't think in terms of men and women, boys and girls. We treated each other as equals. There were no special privileges for women; we were all partisans and we knew that death in war did not spare anyone. Certainly in battle, there was no differentiation between men and women. All our thoughts were concentrated on defeating the enemy. We were all equally committed to destroying the enemy before the enemy could destroy us. The equality in these life-and-death situations fostered a unique understanding amongst us, breaking down the barriers between the sexes. Many times I was appointed to go to an operation in a group in which I

Faye was often the only woman in the group of partisans.

was the only woman. Being the only woman among all those men, sometimes forty or fifty, was not generally of any concern to me. I liked to believe that on our assignments I was seen as a soldier and a colleague, not as a female.

It was rare that I felt self-conscious as the only woman, but it sometimes did occur. Once when we were on the move because of Nazi attacks, we found a broken, abandoned shack. It had no roof, windows or doors, but four walls were still standing. This was a relief for our group since we were experiencing sub-freezing temperatures. At least inside, we would be protected from the cold wind. Our whole group piled into the shack. I was the only woman amongst fifty men. The men squeezed in tightly on the floor and in no time they were all asleep. I felt too shy to climb into the middle of all the men and lie down. Instead I found an empty corner and tucked myself into it as tightly against the two walls as possible to distance myself from the men.

This was a big mistake. After a while, when the shack began to warm up from so much body heat, all the bugs that had been dormant in the walls came to life. Since I was the closest to the corner with two walls touching me, bugs swarmed all over me. I was terrified of bugs; I used to say that for me a bug and a bullet were the same. Though I couldn't see them in the dark, I could feel them crawling all over my body.

I became so agitated that I couldn't sleep. Desperate, I ran outside into minus forty degree weather. Oblivious to the cold, I took off all my clothes and vigorously shook out each piece, one by one. Then I started to rub off my body with snow.

Suddenly I heard a loud voice: "*Parole!*" the password. In my frenzy to clean myself, I had forgotten about the password. Whenever we stopped for a rest there was always a guard around in case of an enemy attack. I couldn't answer, so agitated that the password had slipped my mind. Luckily the guard recognized me and did not fire. He could just as easily have mistaken me for an enemy and pulled the trigger. I got dressed, walked back into the shack and sat down. I didn't dare to lie down any more. I sat far from the corner with my eyes open all through the night.

In my modesty, I had erred. It would have been smarter had I lain down somewhere in the middle among the others. I would at least have had a good night's sleep!

Only during the rare quiet moments — when there was no moving from place to place and no fighting — did the bittersweet tensions between the sexes suddenly arise. Then, particularly after a successful battle, everybody's mood would change. At these times I was noticed as a woman. I received compliments from all around: "so young, so pretty, so nice, so beautiful."

These were the times that I had a chance to think about the personal parts of my life that were missing. I had lost my youth in a painful way. It should have been easy to fall in love with one of the many young, handsome boys. But instead of embracing a loved one, I embraced a rifle.

I felt that for me it would be a crime to fall in love, to have fun, to dance, or to sing. Before the war, as a teenager, I used to love dancing — and I danced a lot. All this was now over for me. I was alone in my mourning, an orphan with her memories. My family was killed, having been tortured and brutalized. I could not allow myself to have fun or be happy. At this time I felt I had survived only to fight for freedom and vengeance. Fighting and helping the wounded — that was my destiny. It was my duty to mourn as long as I lived.

Chapter Eleven

DANGEROUS MISSIONS

*P*ARTISANS WERE EXPECTED to be brave, to stand firm and strong and never to show weakness. We were expected to take incredible risks, to display courage in the face of unbelievable odds, to remain calm and optimistic through nerve-wracking dangers and to rebound quickly from defeat. We had to prepare ourselves for all kinds of difficult environments, harrowing battles and dangerous missions. Otherwise we would be crushed. Sometimes, it was necessary to work out an intricate plan of action, wherein every minute move was pictured beforehand and every decision calculated in advance, so that nothing unexpected would arise. But events did not always work out as planned, in spite of all the bravery, intelligence and strength. Sometimes what would occur was a result of a chance premonition, a stroke of luck or simply fate.

In the spring of 1943, a partisan named Nicolai and I were sent to deliver some important messages to another detachment of our brigade. This detachment was located in a very dangerous area heavily surrounded by Nazis and their collaborators, the local policemen. The commander decided that it would be safer for us to go by boat.

The day before we left had been beautiful and peaceful. As we were preparing our supplies, we felt as if we were setting out on a picnic. We even took the time to have photos taken.

Though this trip was a dangerous one, we were lulled into feeling that everything was idyllic.

At sundown we left our base in our canoe. We travelled not by lake or river, but down a narrow but deep canal. Huge trees, thick bushes and tall grasses reached almost to the sky, making it look like a tunnel of black muddied waters.

Soon after we left, it became dark. It started to rain heavily. The little canoe began to fill up with water. Nicolai steered, while I bailed the water with a wooden board. The storm continued. At times, Nicolai had to stop paddling and help me empty the water from the boat. Though we were uncomfortably wet and the canoe seemed on the point of sinking, it would have been even more dangerous for us to go ashore where we might fall into Nazi hands. We proceeded, neither of us voicing a word of complaint. The storm continued all night. When at last we neared our destination we were exhausted. We consoled each other that in a way we were lucky. Had it not stormed so hard, the swish of the canoe and the cracking of the branches overhead might have brought us to the enemy's attention.

Nicolai was a chivalrous man. He felt sorry for me because I was soaking wet, shivering with cold. When we reached the landing point, he said to me, "You wait in the canoe. I'll go out first and pull the canoe out to the edge, so you won't have to go over your waist in the water. You'll be able to step out onto the ground."

As soon as Nicolai stepped out of the canoe, he touched off a mine. He was blown to pieces in an instant. The grass was so dense and tall that I could not find his body. After such a terrible night in the canoe, we had thought we had made it. Now Nicolai was dead.

I felt terrible — frightened, cold and exhausted. Water dripped from me. By now it had stopped raining, but I was

Faye and Nicolai set out on their tragic mission; spring, 1943.

still drenched. What should I do? I had no dry spare clothing, only what I was wearing. It was not safe to wait and dry my clothes. I took them off, one at a time, and wrung out the water as best I could. I pulled the damp fabric back over my chilled skin.

I was alone in the depths of the forest surrounded by enemies. Where should I go? Which direction should I take?

There were layers of wild growth covering the ground; most of the trees were tremendously tall. To walk even a little ways into the woods would bring me into intense darkness, even at dawn. Wild animals abounded.

I looked up towards the sky. The top of the trees shimmered with beautiful colours. The sun's rays converged to point towards a narrow path. I looked the other way and noticed a second path. There were two paths I could take, each trailing out in a different direction. Which to choose? Which would lead me to the right place? If I took the wrong one, I might easily run into Nazis or the many bandit groups in the forest who opposed us. If I were captured, they would torture me, try to force me to betray my group and then hang me. I found myself on the edge of despair.

At a time like this, it was important not to lose faith. A sixth sense told me not to turn, but to go straight ahead. After the rain, which had lasted all night, the ground was wet and soft, easy to walk on. The path I chose wound along, but where did it lead? Was this the right way? I didn't know. I walked and walked, and it seemed there was no end to the wilderness. I had had nothing to eat all day. How much longer until I reached the base — the right base, I hoped? The sun was high and shone through the trees.

Suddenly, I heard a noise. As I moved closer, I realized it was voices, people talking in Russian. Yes! Yes! This was what I knew. These were partisans! I was in the right place. These were my partisans.

When I approached the group of partisans in my dripping clothes, they looked at me as if I had come from another world. I was so happy that I had forgotten how wet and dirty I was. I had come to the right place! I delivered my messages as I had been ordered to do.

❧

Premonitions visited me many times, frequently before leaving on a dangerous mission. People would say, "This is a dangerous assignment. Chances of coming out alive are very slim. You are risking your life." But I would somehow feel safe and volunteer. Others would say I was crazy, but somehow I knew I would survive. Other times, when everybody said an operation was safe, that there was nothing to be afraid of, my instincts would tell me not to go. Often these were the missions that were not successful and in which hardly anybody survived. I have no explanation for these warnings. It was merely part of my survival instincts.

This particular morning was a very busy one. The boys were moving quietly and furtively. The weather was cold and windy, as March was ending. But such inclemencies did not disturb our preparations. Partisan commanders were going in and out of headquarters. It was obvious that they were planning a mission. When I realized this, I didn't wait but went immediately to headquarters to ask permission to join the mission.

All the officers present wanted to deny my request. "You have been through enough already. You volunteer constantly — too often," they said. "This time the group is going on a very dangerous mission — a suicide mission. We are expecting many casualties. Who knows how many will return alive." Then they added, "It is much safer for you to stay here. This place is quiet and safe."

But as usual, I was persistent: "Please let me go. I want to fight the enemy every chance I have." My whole family appeared again before my eyes, saying, "Take revenge; punish the murderers." I could not remain behind in safety. I made up my mind to go. Eventually, the officers relented. I was permitted to participate once again thanks to my stubborn determination. The commander said, "Okay, get ready."

I knew what "get ready" meant. There was nothing to pack or to take with me except my rifle, a gun and a grenade. "Get ready" meant clean the rifle. Relieved, I sat down on the cold ground under a tree. Cutting off a piece of material from my blouse for a rag, I set to work taking my rifle apart to clean it thoroughly, making sure that it was in good working order. Rifles had to be cleaned daily. Under our heads in the open air on the damp ground all night, they were liable to rust.

At dusk after supper, we left our safe haven. The green tree tops seemed to whisper their regrets that we were leaving. Foreboding shadows stretched out under our feet. For hours we walked in the dark, not along the roads or highways but through the woods where it was much darker because of the tall trees. We could hardly see the sky.

It was still hard for me to keep up with the rest of the group, who were mostly well-trained Soviet soldiers used to walking long hard hours under strenuous conditions. These soldiers possessed an uncanny sense of direction. I had no such experience and felt that one had to be a genius to learn directions in the woods. It was easier in the daytime but at night when it was pitch black I could see nothing. Walking in single file in pitch darkness, the partisans moved along the narrow forest path like shadows, swallowed up by the darkness of night. I tried hard not to lose the person in front of me. If I lost him, I was sure to lose my way.

But I was young and healthy and very persistent. This night I felt fortunate that they had allowed me to come along. At the time I didn't know why. Even though the walk was arduous, a voice inside encouraged me: "Good, good, keep going."

We came to a river that we had to cross. At one time there had been a bridge nearby, but it had been demolished.

To go looking for another bridge was too dangerous. Our enemies were close by. The leader said that this was the only safe place to cross. But how? It was the end of March, still very cold. The river was only half frozen. The centre of the river was solid ice, but at the edges close to the banks the ice had thawed. We had to find a way to get to the solid part of the river and then make it to the other side.

We stopped at the shore. The boys knew what to do and went to work. They chopped off many heavy branches and spread them from the riverbank to where the ice was still thick, building a path of branches. We had to cross one at a time, so the ice would not crack. In the darkness, we couldn't risk walking: each of us had to lie down and roll our way across the branches, holding a rope for safety. It took a few hours, but we all made it safely before daylight.

We continued to our destination. After two days and two nights our assignment was completed. The sound of firing bullets slowly abated. When we reassembled, we found out that this operation really had been a dangerous one: five from our group were missing. Five casualties. We were very upset. We had lost five good fighters and good friends. But this was war. Who knew how much longer the rest of us would remain alive? How many of us would be killed tomorrow?

The sun was setting as we returned to our base. When we arrived, a horrifying picture greeted us. True, we had spies that worked for us, but there were also plenty of traitors who worked for the Nazis. Someone had notified the Nazis that we, the well-armed partisans, had left, and there would be little resistance at our base. They had attacked immediately and killed all those partisans left behind. They had captured and tortured them, cutting their living flesh off in pieces. Such inhuman brutality was characteristic of the Nazi handling of captured partisans.

Once again my instincts had saved me and I had survived. Something had impelled me to leave this presumed haven for a dangerous mission. In spite of everyone's admonition that I was wrong or foolhardy, I had listened to my feelings. Every day I continued to live was a gift from God. Perhaps I was just lucky. Perhaps it was a subliminal awareness of the conditions necessary for survival.

⚯

One of our most important operations — and also one of the most difficult — was to blow up enemy trains. Those heading east to the Russian front brought munitions, military equipment, military personnel and food. Those going west to Germany were loaded with livestock, cows, horses and grain, property that the Nazis had confiscated from farmers and other civilians. The Nazis looted all they conquered, particularly the property of the Jewish people.

We were assembled waiting for the order to strike. Partisans do not wait long. A minute later we heard, "Get up!" We were all on our feet ready to face whatever lay ahead. The commander of the operation gave a brief description of the action about to be undertaken: we were to blow up a railway line. This line was one of the main conduits for reinforcements, military equipment and ammunition for the Nazis on the Eastern Front. The trains were headed east through White Russia. The location for the demolition was about thirty kilometres from our base — not far compared to other operations. We had to reach the tracks after dark. The mission itself would take approximately one hour; we would have enough time to return to our base in complete darkness.

We were accustomed to night excursions. Darkness protected us. Under its cover we advanced along forest paths, over

A Nazi train blown up by the partisans.

ploughed fields, and by the outskirts of villages. We didn't talk much. There was a job to do, and this was how we did it. We stopped to rest only for brief periods. A thick cigarette was rolled, the match lit under a jacket. For a brief moment of calm we sat in a circle taking puffs. It is still so vivid to me: the silence, the burning cigarette passed around, the glowing tip in the palm of the hand. Every mouth drew in a lungful of smoke. One round, then another. The bitter tobacco burned to the tip of its newspaper tube. "Rise!" The command. We were all up and on our way.

The railroad tracks were always heavily patrolled against saboteurs by the Nazis and their collaborators. They forced their slave labourers to cut down the trees on both sides of the tracks, making it dangerous, almost impossible to move in close to the rail lines. Every five hundred metres guard houses loaded with rockets, flares, reflectors and lamps to illuminate the entire length of the track were erected. The Nazis also had trained dogs.

But all this did not stop us from sending their trains flying in the air. When the operation was successful the partisans were able to return safely to base. Failure to return meant that the territory had been mined; every partisan had been killed. Those were the risks that had to be taken. Whether we succeeded or not, the important thing was to keep attacking.

One autumn night, a group of us on assignment emerged from the woods and immediately ran into some train tracks. We knew they were well guarded, but we needed to cross them. The wind was blowing and the trees were whispering as if promising to help us cross undetected. The sky was covered with dark clouds, another source of protection. Our leader told us to cross quietly one by one. Each would cross, and when he made it over safely in the woods on the other side, the next would start. We could make no noise. The enemy was close by.

Altogether there were twenty of us, seventeen boys and three girls. Fourteen had made it to the other side. The fifteenth tripped. His rifle dropped on the iron tracks with a loud clatter. In an instant, midnight turned into noon. The Nazis filled the sky with rockets and flares. Frightened to death, we lay flat and motionless on the ground. For several hours we did not move. We were too few in number to take on hundreds of Nazis. Nevertheless, we kept our rifles in readiness. Time dragged but not one of us moved a muscle. If we had to sneeze, we were told to rub our nose and sneeze quietly. Eventually everything quieted down. The flares stopped going off. It became night again. The Nazis probably thought that it had been a wild animal that made the noise. We resumed our journey.

When our group successfully returned to base, we were met with stares. I had been presumed killed in crossing the tracks because other groups crossing after us had found my hat. The hat had been a sign to them that I was missing. Of course they were happy to see me alive, and I didn't even know that my hat had been lost.

~

The Nazi police station was located in a single large house on the outskirts of Mikashevich. The policemen were local traitors; we used to call them "German dogs." Those forty-five Nazi collaborators gave us a lot of trouble. They were constantly ambushing us. Now the time had come to destroy their headquarters and put an end to them.

A group of ten partisans was organized to attack the collaborators. I was assigned to join them. My job was to wait at the outskirts of town to help with any casualties that arose. It was clear that ten against forty-five was risky; the chances of accomplishing our mission were slim. Planning was crucial. After various considerations, we decided to employ a ruse. We concluded that if the local boys were volunteers for the Nazis, they did not have many brains in their heads. There was a good chance we would be able to trick them by exploiting their ignorance of the German language. This was the basis of our carefully worked-out plan.

Nine of the ten partisans got dressed as Nazi officers, complete with boots, coats, hats, belts and even scarves. The remaining partisan dressed in civilian clothes: he was to act as the interpreter. The ironic part was that this "interpreter" could not speak German either.

In the middle of the night, all ten disguised partisans walked straight into the Nazi police station. The "interpreter" stretched out his arm in salute and loudly greeted the police, "*Heil* Hitler!" Then he said in Russian, which the police understood, that the nine Nazi officers had come unannounced for a surprise inspection of their weapons and of their preparedness to fight the partisans. This was an order from the *Gebiets-kommissar*, the Nazi high command. Since the collaborators could not speak German, they didn't ask many questions. All they answered was "*Heil* Hitler!"

Then the interpreter said, "The Nazi *Wehrmacht* has ordered a check of your firearms. Put all of your rifles and guns on the tables. The officers are going to check them for cleanliness."

"*Jawohl!*" they answered. And the collaborators took the rifles from their shoulders and the guns from their belts. Their next order was to take out the bullets so the Nazis could see how clean they were. As soon as all the firearms were lying on the table unloaded, a shout rang out in Russian, "*Ruki na verch!*" [Hands up.] The collaborators were shot without the loss of a single partisan. That is how ten partisans overcame forty-five traitors.

❧

All that I went through to survive other Jews also experienced. There are accounts of suffering far worse than my own. I, after all, survived all my dangerous missions, while thousands of Jewish boys and girls fell in battle, losing their lives heroically fighting for freedom. These heroes were buried in the woods with no monuments, stones or signs. Nobody will ever know what they went through and where they lie. The woods in White Russia are filled with the dead. The ground is drenched in Jewish blood.

These young people perished as though they had never been alive. The ground would be soft one day with new graves. A few weeks later, it would be covered with newly grown grass, weeds and field flowers, as if nothing had happened. Only the tall trees with their long, dark shadows whispered to the wind, "Let the world know, spread the news all over. Tell the world what is going on!" Their torture, their suffering, their bravery demand remembrance.

I remember well the brave spirit of one particular Jewish boy whose death I witnessed. I can still see him lying there on the damp ground. A young partisan, about eighteen years old, he had been hit by a bullet that exploded in his stomach. He only had a few minutes to live and he knew it. Though he was in terrible pain, he did not complain. He asked me for a favour, wanting me to call over the little twelve year old Jewish boy who worked in the designated "kitchen" area in the woods.

I ran to the kitchen and called little David to the dying young partisan. David came immediately. He looked into the eyes of the wounded man. In a weak voice that was barely audible the dying partisan said, "David, I want you to have my rifle. Take it over from me, and now you continue to fight. Take revenge for our people. Continue what I could not accomplish." He paused, then added, "Good luck to you. I am leaving this world. I am going to join my family." With these words he closed his eyes. He was one of the thousands of others who lost their lives in battle and were buried in the White Russian ground.

From that day on little David joined the resistance lines with a rifle in his hands, just like the grown-ups, like an experienced soldier. He fulfilled the dying partisan's request. Of course David, too, had his reasons for fighting. He too was an orphan, the sole survivor of his family. He reminded me of my little brother Boruch who, had he lived, might also have become a brave young partisan fighter.

Chapter Twelve

BITTER SEASONS

*T*HE WINTER OF 1943 was particularly cold. Record-breaking freezing temperatures and sharp eastern winds heralded a heavy snowfall from the low clouds. For the partisans, it was an extremely difficult time. The Nazis attacked us daily and we were constantly forced to change our location.

Whenever our base was attacked or we heard rumours of an enemy blockade, we would scatter in small groups, dispersing in different directions. Each group would then form a new interim base until things became safer again. At that point we would all return to our original headquarters base, this being the designated gathering point where we would reconvene with the rest of our brigade.

This was our way of life month after month that winter. The momentum of our daily life in those days is still very vivid to me. While we were on the move, there was no time to dig the bunkers we usually built for shelter in the snow or in the ground. Especially in the winter, these bunkers provided us with a bit of warmth and comfort while we slept. We slept in the snow. Sometimes in the morning we would find ourselves frozen to the ground. We would scarcely have managed to make a flimsy shelter from branches when the order would come to move on again.

While news of the Nazi defeat at Stalingrad in January had greatly encouraged us, by February it seemed possible that the Soviet forces would lose the territory on the Eastern Front that they had so painfully won. By mid-March, the Nazi forces seemed to have reversed all the Soviet gains. Could no power in the world stand against the Nazis? The contrast between our lot and that of our enemy was painful. We in the woods would go for days without food or a change of clothes. Ambushes had to be conducted to obtain clean garments. We did not have a roof over our heads, nor a blanket with which to cover ourselves. Many times we lay down to sleep hungry on the wet, rough ground, in the cold. For the two years I was with the partisans I never slept in a bed.

In terms of supplies, the situation was equally bad. We were always short of firearms. Some of our rifles were rusted and old. We had no cars, no tanks or other armoured vehicles, certainly no planes. There were few doctors and no hospitals. We were always in urgent need of medical supplies.

We thought with envy of our enemy's situation. They were well equipped, with good weapons and an endless supply of ammunition. Their firearms were the best, as were their cars, tanks and planes. They were a strong army and they were determined to destroy us, since we were an increasing threat. They had doctors for their wounded and no shortage of medical supplies. They had food, good clothing to wear, good boots. At night, lying on the cold ground, we would think of them asleep in beds with pillows in warm, dry houses. Those well-organized murderers had everything they wanted.

We may have been poorly equipped, but our main weapon, personal courage, was in abundant supply. We fought hard and with surprising success, knowing that surrender meant torture and death. There was no other way to survive. We had to win. The Jewish partisans in particular revealed great internal power, but we often paid with our lives for our unfettered will to fight.

And there were times, especially in that dreadful winter, when we became fed up with this way of life. How could we not long to be free, to live like regular people, like human beings? Hadn't we had enough suffering, enough exhausting, sleepless nights?

❦

It was near the end of that seemingly interminable winter of 1943 that we found a camp which seemed relatively safe and stable. For five weeks we were at last able to stay in one place. The ground was frozen and covered with snow so it was impossible to know what type of terrain lay under the cover of snow.

Eventually the harsh winter began to subside. The snow melted little by little each day. The temperature began to hover above the freezing mark. We were looking forward at last to some warm weather and sunshine. Soon we would need to move our base again.

The night had been warm. We woke to find that all the snow was gone, and the ground was wet and bare. With the snow cover gone, for the first time we were able to see the terrain. We were camped on an island encircled by impenetrable mud and swamps. With the thaw, what had been firm ground was revealed as quicksand. We were in real danger now. If the enemy found that we were stuck here, they could easily surround and kill us all. If we were discovered, we would not be able to hold our position for long, nor would we be able to escape or to defend ourselves. In no time we would run out of bullets.

Faye with Ivan Vasilievich on the plank
bridge over the quicksand; spring, 1943.

There was no time to lose. We had to find a way out. We had to lay a provisional bridge from the island to the firm ground beyond the quicksand, a distance of a few hundred feet. We cut down trees and lay them, one after the other, as planks. By means of this makeshift bridge we walked off the island. It was not an easy job, since we had no saws or axes. But we worked very hard and made it in time, before informers had a chance to notify the Nazis of our predicament.

～

Because the Hebrew calendar does not correspond to the secular calendar, during the partisan years I never knew when the Jewish holidays were: neither the Jewish New Year, Yom

Kippur, Passover, or any other holiday. The sole exception was Passover 1943. When I had been briefly reunited with my brother Kopel the previous fall, just before we were forced to go our separate ways Kopel had given me the exact corresponding date. This was the only time I was able to observe a Jewish holiday during my two years among the partisans.

Passover 1943 was certainly nothing like the way it had been at home. There was no special dinner, no prayers at synagogue and, most painfully of all, no family with whom to celebrate. Life had changed drastically and none of my former rituals existed any more. The only means I could think of to observe the holiday was to eat neither bread nor soup.

Soup and bread were our mainstay. Only when things were calm did our cook have the opportunity to cook a more elaborate meal for us. An important aspect in the observance of Passover is to refrain from eating bread. The eating of pork is forbidden to Jews at all times. Our soup was normally cooked with flour and pork. Though I was forced to eat pork during my years among the partisans, I made a commitment to myself not to eat pork for these eight days of Passover. This meant not joining the group at dinnertime.

Eating together was a communal ritual among the partisans. We all ate together, ten to twelve partisans sitting on the ground around a big basin of soup. Everyone reached for their spoons, which were always stored in our boots for safety. Then we would take turns dipping into the basin for a spoonful of soup. We had no individual bowls; we all ate together from one basin.

After the meal, "dessert" was a communal cigarette. One of the comrades would fish a piece of newspaper out of his pocket; another would find a little bit of tobacco, a cigarette was rolled up, and everybody inhaled a puff. The cigarette went around in a circle several times until the end. We shared one cigarette for ten to twelve people. This was our moment of togetherness, our quiet time together.

Now it was Passover. I wasn't able to join the meal nor to tell anyone why. Among the Soviet partisans, I was, after all, supposed to act like a communist, not a believer in religion. In addition, not everybody knew that I was Jewish. I was supposed to be like one of them; we were all comrades. I decided to keep my observance a secret.

Every day of that week, I went to the kitchen and got a few potatoes to bake in the hot ashes of the campfire. For eight days I lived on baked potatoes. This was not difficult for me. However, the boys became uneasy when I failed to join them, worried something was wrong with me. Why wasn't I eating? They didn't know about the potatoes. I made up all kinds of excuses and managed to observe Passover for the full eight days in my very own way. One thing was sure; I was glad when Passover was over. No doubt it would have been much easier for me if I hadn't known the date of this Passover, just as I had been ignorant of the dates of all other Jewish holidays.

⤝

One day I found myself alone, away from the group, walking in the woods. This was in the springtime, after a rain. Moisture gleamed on the grass and the scent coiled slowly into the air. The ground was soft, and the greenery was light in colour. Leaves and flowers opened in beautiful colours. Everything smelled so fresh. I suddenly remembered how I had always been moved by nature, had always had the camera in my hands, looking for beautiful scenery to photograph and then to paint. Everything was gorgeous; the birds were singing. I took a deep breath. It was like a dream, as if I were back to a time before the war.

The world was still beautiful, but my family and so many other Jewish people couldn't admire this beauty any more. How could I still enjoy it? The dreams I used to have, youthful dreams, where were they now? They drowned in the rivers of innocent blood. There no longer was a safe place where I could dream about a life of peace and quiet. My life was filled with violence, brutality and terror. Thinking about all this, I had to pause for a while just to regain control over my emotions.

❦

Our difficult times continued well into that summer of 1943. Again we could not remain long in one place. We were continuously on the move, with little food, little water, not enough sleep and steady enemy attacks.

After a rainy summer night, we were soaked through, with no dry clothes to change into and no shelter from the elements. The clothes we wore had to dry while we wore them, with the help of the sun or wind. And when it had been raining for days, the cold wet from our clothes penetrated the whole body.

When it was hot, on the other hand, we would often become dehydrated. Especially when we were on the move — and we were tired, hot and thirsty, our throats parched — we could not stop to look for water often, lest the enemy locate our position. There were few lakes and it was hard to find a river. Water was a precious commodity at those times, even more important than food. Sometimes we would come across little patches of dirty rain water, alive with bugs and worms. It did not matter — we were so thirsty we would drink anything. This was when a hat came in handy. I would fill my hat with this infested water, then spread a piece of gauze from my first aid kit over one end of my hat and drink the water through this make-shift strainer. I didn't know what I was swallowing, but at the moment I didn't care. After my drink, I would feel refreshed, stronger and able to continue our journey.

Sometimes I wondered whether it was easier for us during the summer or the winter. The advantage during winter was that the ground was frozen and we were able to take short cuts. No need to detour around rivers, swamps or quicksand. A sleigh and horse were considerably quieter than a horse and wagon, whose clatter on the bumpy summer roads could be heard for miles. In the winter, snowstorms would cover our footsteps, as did the spring rain. But after the rain stopped, the unpaved roads would be so muddy that it was difficult to walk; the mud clung to our boots, which sank deep with each step; we just dragged our feet along. When the ground was firm in good weather, we would often have to walk backwards, so the enemy, seeing our footsteps, would go after us in the opposite direction.

※

The situation in the forest gradually changed. By the autumn of 1943, the partisan movement had grown strong. There were now hundreds of detachments and thousands of well-organized partisans. Trained soldiers had been parachuted from the Soviet Union in order to organize and help our brigades. The loyalties of the local populations that surrounded us in the forests were changing to our side. People began to believe that the Nazis might lose the war. Even though officially we were still behind Nazi lines, the Nazis were only able to move in reinforced columns in the woods. The forest was now known as partisan territory.

Though none of us could have known this for sure at the time, the tide of the war was indeed beginning to turn. In May 1943, Allied forces had defeated the Nazis in Tunisia. Throughout the summer of 1943, Allied bombing of Germany and Italy had been devastating. In July, Mussolini had been arrested; in August, Sicily had fallen to the Allies; in October, Italy declared war on Germany. Closer to home, the Soviet advances on the Eastern Front, despite their cost, had been spectacular. Our own actions were of increasing effect on the enemy, and morale was now high.

One day in the fall of 1943 our detachment came upon a herd of horses — one for almost every fighter. To me, the benefit was not particularly obvious. Although a number of the boys knew all about horses, their personalities and idiosyncrasies, how some were docile while others would not even let you come close to them, I myself was totally ignorant about these subtleties of the personalities of horses.

The boys decided this was a good time to play a joke on me, to have some fun. They called me over and offered what they said was a fine horse. I climbed into the saddle, not knowing that this particular horse had a wild disposition. As soon as I sat on him, he began to gallop and ran towards a tree, trying to throw me off. Holding on as tightly as I could, I was terrified. Meanwhile the boys were having their laugh.

Miraculously, Ivan Vasilievich seemed to appear out of nowhere. He ran towards the horse, managed to grab its reins, and stopped it. I jumped off, relieved. It was good to have a friend nearby. I picked another horse, a more docile one that I could ride safely.

❦

Despite the sometimes mischievous companionship of my fellow partisans, there were times I felt very alone. I remember one day in particular. I found myself among tall, dense trees with widespread branches. The branches of one tree overlapped its neighbours so thickly that I could hardly see the grey, cloudy and heavy sky hanging overhead. Each time I looked up through the branches, I felt as though the sky were getting lower and heavier. Finally it started to rain. The rain poured down in bucketfuls, and the weather become stormy and windy. At first, the trees protected me from the rain, but after a while, they became laden with water which began to pour down from the trees. I sat down under a tree on the sodden ground and pressed myself against a tree trunk for protection. I covered my face with my hands to wait it out. There was nothing I could do, no place to hide, no place to run or look for something to cover myself with. This was the forest and I had no place to go. After long hours, the sky slowly lightened. It was still drizzling, but it had stopped pouring. I was soaked through. The wet clothes and cold wind chilled my body. When I got up, I felt how cold I really was. The water ran off my body.

I couldn't help but think how lucky the people were who had a roof over their heads, a warm house, a bed, a warm meal or a cup of hot water. But not I. I didn't have all this luxury, couldn't even dream or think about such things. All I knew was that I was wet and had no dry clothes to change into. I looked up to the sky again. Perhaps the sun would come out from the clouds. The only thing that could help now would be the sun; the sun would warm me up and dry my clothes. But where was the sun? Still covered with dark clouds. It was still drizzling. No such luck in getting dry soon. I felt my throat close up and began to shake from the cold. There was no dry place, nobody to complain to. I mustn't make a fuss about this. I had to show everyone a happy face. Every good thing, a normal life — all this was in the past. Now everything was ruined, or burnt; everyone was murdered. My life consisted of swamps, water, ice and freezing cold weather; my lot a rifle and a bed on the hard ground winter and summer. I was not allowed to be sick — there was no medicine. The water I drank was full of bugs, but nothing happened to me. I was stronger than steel.

⚜

The news had spread quickly through our base: eleven spies had been captured alive. What a sensation. Everyone thought to themselves: Who were they? Where did they come from? Could it be true that all of them were spies? Nobody knew and nobody had the guts to ask. We never asked too many questions.

In the morning, I was called to headquarters. The commander wanted to see me. Three of them were sitting, waiting: the commander, the *nachalnik shtaba* and the commissar. The commissar said, "Fanya, do you have a strong heart?"

"Yes, Comrade Commissar, I have a strong heart." Of course this was my answer. I couldn't say that I was weak; I didn't know why he was asking. Then the *nachalnik shtaba* said, "Good! You will stab." I felt my stomach turn inside out. Not showing my feelings, I answered like a soldier, "Yes, Comrade *Nachalnik Shtaba.*" I looked at the commander and he said, "You are a good partisan. You work hard, you take pictures, you help the wounded, and you volunteer for operations. We would like to honour you. You will be one of the partisans who will stab the eleven spies. Tomorrow at six o'clock in the morning, be in this location." He showed me where, about two hundred feet to the side where the tall trees

175

were. That was to be the site for the stabbing.

I left with a shudder. What should I do? I couldn't kill in cold blood. It was one thing to fight as a soldier. But for me this was different. For some partisans, killing was a pleasure or at least a way of life. But not for me; I was not a killer. I could not confront cruelty and savagery with more of the same. I preferred my work as a nurse, helping the wounded.

This was a dilemma for me which I could not share with my partisan superiors. I had an idea: I would show up a little late. I knew how eager others would be to have the "honour" of stabbing the spies.

When I arrived about fifteen minutes later I could still hear the desperate cries of the eleven spies who had already been stabbed. They were still moving. As I came to the site, I was approached by a few partisans who apologized for having done the job themselves. They had been too anxious to wait.

I left as soon as a could and hid myself in a bunker. Alone, I burst into tears, an action not in keeping with the seasoned partisan I was. But my old wounds were not yet healed, and now they were scratched open again. All the pain came back to me. I saw not those eleven dead spies, but my own mother in her death throes, my father in a pool of blood, my sisters and my brothers with bullets through them. I was convulsed with fear.

I didn't know how long I was like this until I heard a familiar voice calling me. It was Ivan Vasilievich. He comforted me and I stopped crying. He promised he wouldn't tell anybody that I had been crying. I was ashamed to cry; this was not the partisan way.

❦

I served among the partisans with a rifle in my hands, went to sleep with the rifle under my head. People who didn't share

*Faye with her unit. The man on the
left of Faye is the* nachalnik shtaba.

this experience don't understand how I could do it. Sometimes I have felt the unasked question: "You don't look like a killer. How could you have been a partisan soldier?" I am not a killer. I never considered myself one. A partisan soldier is not a killer. A partisan fights for peace and justice.

What I saw the Nazis perpetrate made me hungry for justice. I once witnessed a horrible instance of the inhuman torture the Nazis used. We were on the outskirts of a village. Before entering, we had sent in a scout. He reported that about twenty Nazis had just left, so we decided to enter the village to search for some food. When we reached the first house this shocking picture awaited us. A young woman in her twenties lay half naked under a tree in front of the house.

Her tongue had been cut out and her breasts cut off. Beside her was a dead baby. Pools of blood lay all around. The woman was somehow still alive and she made feeble gestures for help. She wanted to live....

A scene such as this stays forever in one's mind and made me long for justice and revenge on the Nazis. I wanted to seek out and strike at the enemy. At the same time, I wanted to live in peace, free from such bestiality. There was no choice but to become tougher, stronger, with more energy and more eagerness to end the war.

Chapter Thirteen

A MAJOR BLOCKADE

W INTER 1944. ANOTHER cold winter day brought its Russian storms, with driving snow, winds and frost. This did not stop our offensive; on the contrary, we fought with great eagerness. Our group had an assignment to go east to attack a Nazi garrison and obtain vital supplies. I volunteered to go along. I was again out of medical supplies; I needed to obtain clean bandages for the wounded partisans. Usually, if the circumstances allowed, I would cleanse the wounds and change the dressings every second day.

I was going to wear my leather boots which were in perfect condition, but everybody said, "Leave the boots here and wear the *valenkes*. Your feet will be safer from frostbite." *Valenkes* were boots made out of felt that were much warmer than leather boots. I listened and put on the *valenkes*.

We had to pass through a number of villages to reach our destination. We thought that it was a safe area. It was quiet; we heard no shooting. But when we entered one village at night, the people were astonished to see us. "What are you doing here? There are Nazis all over now, in the thousands, coming this way. You're lucky that you're alive. They are at this moment in the village which you just left. They'll reach us here any time now." Hearing this, we departed immediately.

We could not fight such large numbers. We proceeded walking to the next village. It, too, was full of Nazis. By this time we were hungry and tired and it was very cold, but there was no time to eat, and certainly no time to rest. The same thing occurred in the next village. We kept moving from one village to the next.

We found out that the Nazis had organized a massive assault on the partisans in the vicinity, whose increasing strength was proving a greater and greater threat. Nazi troops advanced shoulder to shoulder along a line of five kilometres. They had decided to get rid of the partisans once and for all. We were told that this blockade totalled seventy-five thousand Nazis and their collaborators. They were destroying everything in their path, setting villages and farms aflame and killing innocent civilians. During this operation, they burned twenty-eight villages to the ground and killed thousands of the civilian population: mostly White Russians, farmers and local peasants. The villages and farms became cemeteries.

The Nazis propaganda announced on huge posters that they had killed many thousands of partisans. This was not true. In reality those they killed were the area's civilian population. The partisans escaped in time, fleeing in all directions. Our group didn't know exactly what was happening. We had left our base only a few hours before the raids began. We kept going and weren't aware that we were always just ahead of the enemy. We would walk out of one village and the Nazis would walk in. We were just lucky. It was a miracle.

But one thing we did know: we had to keep going. That first night we made about forty kilometres. After that night we kept moving from one place to another, day in and day out. It was cold in the daytime and the nights were even colder, in the twenties or thirties below zero. From time to time we heard the howling of wolves in the distance.

This major Nazi raid forced most of the partisan detachments from their bases and scattered them all over the woods
in White Russia. My group was now trying to return to its
base. On the way, we met many smaller groups, but none
from our brigade.

It was chaotic and frightening. There were many bandits,
many enemy groups in the woods who were collaborating
with the Nazis against the Soviet partisans. We never knew
who or where the enemy was. There were instances of partisan groups, not knowing who was approaching, shooting at
each other. In many cases, people shot without asking questions. If a partisan or a Russian boy happened to be wearing a
Nazi uniform, he was taken for a Nazi and killed. After a raid
there was no control, no contact and of course, no tele-
phones, no messengers or communication.

Our group wanted to return to our base. It was a long
way; we had to cross railway lines, rivers, highways and to
pass through villages that were heavily guarded by the Nazis
and their collaborators. Luckily, for the time being the
ground was still frozen. There was no need to detour around
swamps and we were able to take short cuts.

So far, our group had been lucky. We ran into another
group that had not been as fortunate. I cannot forget that
detachment of sixty-five partisans, all of them heavily frostbitten. It was a frightening scene. Surrounded by the enemy,
they had been forced to lie flat on the frozen ground in temperatures about thirty to forty degrees below zero, immobile.
The moment a partisan raised his head, he was shot. They
somehow had managed to hold their position, and fought
back. To surrender would mean torture and then hanging.
They held their own for three days and three freezing nights.
Finally another group of partisans came to their rescue. By
the time the group of sixty-five were freed, all had incurred

heavy frostbite. Some had their ears frostbitten, some hands, fingers, legs, toes and noses.

When we came upon them, their situation was desperate. Their bodies were rotting away. With every passing day, the frostbite had spread. It was like rot in an apple that begins in one little spot and spreads day by day until the whole apple has rotted. The smell was terrible, entirely different from a bullet wound gushing fresh blood. When they asked me to help of course I did what I could. Some I could not help at all; the gangrene had gone too far and the conditions made surgery impossible.

Seeing the suffering of those I could not help — the dying, those who were losing their arms, legs, faces, or ears — was devastating. Though I was in despair at my helplessness, I could not show it. I had to appear cheerful, to smile encouragement, tell them that they would be all right. I felt a great deal for each one of them. It was all too easy to picture myself in their place.

For the two weeks my group and I stayed with them, I tended them and helped them in every way I could. Then we were ordered to leave. My patients understood that an order had to be obeyed. Though they didn't complain or protest, they cried. Tears ran across their faces. Can anybody imagine the suffering, the pain they went through?

We were passing by a village when a farm girl came running to us crying, calling me doctor. I don't know how the local people found out about us so quickly. The girl said that the Nazis had shot her father but he was still alive. She wanted my help. It wasn't far, so I went with her to the farm house. I had nothing with me, no medication. I had used up all my supplies for the frostbitten partisans. I asked the daughter to boil some water, and I sterilized a strip of bed sheet. I added a little salt, which was the main medication when there was nothing better. I washed the wound with the salted, sterilized water, covered it with a piece of sterilized dressing, and bandaged the wound with the sheet strips. It was the best I could do. That done, I left to rejoin my group.

We kept moving through the forest, which stretched for great distances through this part of Polesie. The trees were tall and dense, blocking the sun, giving a dark, grey light even at noon time. The twilight hours were long. For the partisan in the forest, darkness was a friend. We felt safer in the dark. As long as the earth had not donned its cloak of darkness, we dared not leave the thickness of the forest. I had long forgotten the normal comforts of life at home in a town with houses and streets, had forgotten what it was like to walk freely on the sidewalks, lie in a warm bed, get up in the morning, and go to sleep at night. Now, most of the time, we walked at night and slept and rested in the day. The wolves were our friends. I used to be afraid of wolves, but no longer. Now I knew that wolves fled human activity. If there were wolves about, no Nazis would be found.

I recalled an incredible incident a few months earlier. The night had been bitterly cold, the snow and ice squeaking under our feet. We were freezing, but kept walking uncomplaining in silence. Every tired step plunged in and out of endless snow. Suddenly we noticed the glimmer of lights in the distance. We looked at each other hopefully. Maybe this was a farm house; maybe there were no Nazis. We would be able to step in a house and warm up, at least for a short time. We would have given anything to be inside a house, to warm our hands and feet. Our hands especially were cold, holding the metal rifles. The adrenaline flowed; we started to walk faster. The glow of the lights became clearer. Our mood improved; we had hope. We walked and walked, but somehow did not get any closer to the source of the fire. In fact, it kept receding. Finally, it disappeared completely. Only then did we realize what the lights were: the eyes of wolves. Like cats', wolves' eyes shine at night. Our dreams of a warm house flew away with the cold wind. One good thing did come to our mind; at least if there were wolves ahead, there would be no enemies. We could proceed in safety.

⚬

During the period of the blockade, we could not proceed along the highways or good roads; ours was the narrow path through the swamps where Nazi feet would not reach. The Nazis would not want to step into mud up to their waists. This we had to do many times to be on the safe side. We were constantly trying to join up with our own brigade so we wouldn't be taken for deserters. It was against regulations to unite with other groups. We had to look for our own commander and our own brigade. This was our task now.

As soon as the ground thawed my *valenkes* were useless. In the daytime they were soaked all through and became very heavy. At night the temperature went down below the freezing point. Everything that thawed during the day turned to ice at night. Since I slept on the ground, the *valenkes* would freeze to my feet. I banged my feet against each other, the *valenkes* clinging heavily like pieces of ice. It became impossible to wear them. Finally I threw them away, and tied my feet with rags. I added pieces of wood to the bottom for soles, because without wood the rags would not last very long. Walking day and night, sometimes ten or twenty kilometres at a time, those rags on my feet were a misery.

Another couple of weeks passed, with our group sleeping on the wet ground. We proceeded further. The days were much warmer, but the nights were still cold. There was never a special place to sleep: wherever we stopped for a rest, there we slept. The wetter the ground and the deeper in the woods, the safer we were. I no longer cared if I got wet, dirty, and covered with mud.

After six weeks of struggling, our group finally was able to rejoin the other detachments of our brigade. Our units were established now in the same old place, back in the depth of the forest and swamps within twenty-five kilometres of the Nazi regiments. It had been a long and difficult journey to come back to our base; one miracle after another had kept us alive.

The bitter winter had come to an end. Just to the south of us, the Soviet offensive from January through April 1944 had pushed the Nazis out of the Ukraine. By mid-May, the area south of the Pripet River and as far west as Tarnopol was occupied by Soviet forces. The thaw brought a brief, temporary halt to the Soviet offensive.

It was spring of 1944. The snow had melted. The rock-hard frozen ground began to thaw and each day was a little warmer. The fresh air and the sweet scent of spring filled our lungs. The surface of the earth took on a green blanket, the trees and bushes turned green. It was beautiful, so pleasant to look at, the light green spring colours all over the woods, the flowers showing their lovely shades. The birds began singing. Sometimes you could see a few of them gathered on a fresh grave of a partisan as though they were elegizing the hero or heroine whose life had been lost in battle.

Yes, everything was beautiful, but the beauty was flawed. Something was terribly wrong. Reality was coming back to me. Danger and death were still all around me. I was used to that. But in my six weeks away, something had changed. Back in my own brigade, I didn't feel the friendliness and devotion I had grown used to. I became aware that there were so few Jewish partisans among us now. What had happened? Where were they all? Why did I feel strange looks? I myself hadn't changed during my six weeks away. I felt I had done so much, so many good things in that terrible time. I had helped so many of the wounded during our wanderings. The frostbitten partisans had cried at my departure. Why the cold greetings now? I had to find out. After a few days had passed, I came across a Jewish boy and asked him, "What happened? What is going on? Where are the Jewish boys and girls?"

He hung his head. "Most of the Jewish partisans were dismissed, sent away from the units into Nazi jaws because they did not have rifles." The order had been given by partisan headquarters. The partisans did not want the enemy to think that so many partisans were without rifles. A poorly armed opponent would be attacked with a stronger decisive force. The easiest solution was to expel the Jews. As always, when the Jews were not needed, they were no longer wanted.

With me in the same brigade was an "older" Jewish man. He was really not old, maybe fifty at the most, but since I was so young, to me he was old. I called him "the old man." When he found out that our own partisans had expelled the Jews from their ranks, he wanted to do something to help. Some of our Jewish former partisans had survived and were hiding defenceless in the woods. One day, the "old man" called me aside. He had an idea about how to get the partisans to take the Jews back, or, if worst came to worst, to allow them to defend themselves. He wanted to know my opinion. I asked what he would like to do. I knew that we were not in a position to do much. He said he would like to write a letter to America, to ask the Jewish organizations to somehow get rifles to the Jews who were hiding in the woods. That way, the Soviet partisans wouldn't be obliged to support or accept them, and the Jews would have the opportunity to defend themselves and fight the enemy, just like the Russians.

I was very impressed. I felt honoured that this older man was sharing his hopes with me, that he wanted my opinion. I thought for a while, then I said, short and definitively, "No! Don't do it! It is too risky." I knew the Russians very well. The best way to survive was to keep quiet and not to talk. I warned him, but he did not take my advice. He told some of the gentiles his ideas about the letter. Since there was no mail service in the woods, the letter would have to be sent out by messenger. He told them exactly what he wanted to write. The next day he was stabbed to death.

This good man had wanted to save the lives of many defenceless, starving people. The excuse for the stabbing was that if the letter to America asking for firearms were written, the enemy might find out and conclude that the partisans were weak and under-armed. The Nazis would then be more aggressive and the fighting would intensify.

Such incidents happened often. For every one I have described, many more remain untold. The life I had and the experiences I went through are impossible to depict fully on paper.

❧

The routine of a peaceful day reigned that spring day of 1944 at our base. Then suddenly, around noon, a Nazi helicopter dove down at us. We all ran for the nearest bushes. I flung myself down on the ground and lay there, my arms covering my head, petrified. When I finally looked up it seemed as though the helicopter was right on top of me, that each bullet would smash directly into my head. The bullets flew like hail, like sparkling rain. The helicopter was so low over us that I saw the faces of the Nazis, their machine guns pointed to the ground, showering us with bullets. We lay there helpless.

Returning their fire would have been futile because we had no anti-aircraft weapons or firearms heavy enough to shoot down the helicopter. Our rifles could do nothing. Hiding was our only option. The enemy had known exactly where our base was located. The Nazi collaborators, their informers, had directed them to our exact location.

The air was full of bullets. Immobilized, I was terrified. Which bullet would get me? How much longer would I remain alive — a minute, a second? I held my breath, not moving a muscle. Would I be killed outright or wounded? No! I would rather be dead than tortured. Each second seemed a lifetime. Suddenly, it was over. The sky cleared; the helicopter was gone. I started to breathe. All over the ground lay dead and wounded partisans. I heard voices calling for help from all directions. My fear vanished. My only thoughts were to look for bandages. Before I knew it I was up and running, attending the wounded, one after the other. I was alive and my work again lay ahead of me.

❦

Despite the tensions from within and without, we had moments of peace. When things were calm, those of us who were left would sit around a burning campfire, the flame casting a glow on our faces. Each held a rifle, loaded, freshly cleaned, and ready for defence. Someone would begin to sing a partisan song, and we would all join in. One song was called, "Oh, What Joy When the War Will Be Over." Another song described the martyrdom of a young partisan on horseback who was loved by a pretty girl.

I sang also, but my mind was not with the song. When the war was over would I have a place where I belonged? Who would wait at the station to meet me? Who would celebrate freedom with me? There would be no homecoming parades for me, no time even to mourn the dead. If I did survive, where would I return? My home and my town had been razed to the ground, its people killed. I was not in the same situation as the colleagues surrounding me. I was a Jew and a woman. Sitting around the campfire, I said nothing. I just sang along. When I was with them, I acted like one of them. I didn't place myself in the future. If I were to begin to think about the future, my heart would break.

Chapter Fourteen

LIBERATION

W ITH EVERY PASSING DAY, the front line came closer and closer to partisan territory. Sometimes we could hear the distant thuds of heavy artillery. We knew that it was the Soviet army because among the partisans there were no such heavy firearms. Ours were the type that could be carried over our shoulders. It was clear that the Nazis were about to be driven from our territory and that the partisan war was coming to an end.

After the temporary halt for the spring thaw, the Soviet offensive resumed in late June. Their advance was implacable, despite bitter resistance from the Nazis. On July 2, 1944, the First and Third Belorussian Fronts of the Soviet army converged on Minsk. The First Belorussian Front cut the railway line between Minsk and Baranovich. On July 3, Minsk was liberated. The front line was now to our west. Our base and its surrounding territory had at last been scoured of Nazi troops. The Soviets claimed 400,000 Nazi dead and 158,000 taken prisoner. The victory was overwhelming. The partisan forces in our area had been fighting from June 1941 to July 1944: three long hard years of struggle and suffering.

Our brigade entered Pinsk, where we liberated the city. On the day of liberation, I was awarded a medal from the

Soviet government for fighting heroically as a partisan during the war. Then our brigade was demobilized and we dispersed. We were free to leave the woods and live like human beings again.

Now my most serious self-questioning began. Though the situation was still dangerous for Jews, I had to give back my rifle, my gun, and the grenade — my constant companions throughout the last two years. I felt a loss of identity. What would I do with my new-found freedom? Freedom to do what? To go where? In the woods with the partisans, I had rarely thought about the future. There was never the quiet or the time to think. Daily battles, ambushes, attacks, minding the wounded, wandering from one place to another, surviving the freezing cold winters with no shelter — this had occupied all my attention. I had been totally focused on survival and revenge. Resistance had been an act of desperation, since hope for survival was slim. I had had no confidence that at the end of the war I would still be alive.

The fighting for me had come to an end and I was alive and found myself free. Yet this was the lowest point in my life; I saw no future for myself. My Russian partisan friends celebrated liberation with singing and dancing. They shared their happiness by telling funny stories about their parents, their brothers and sisters. They spoke about the festive receptions they could expect when they arrived home, the victory parades to which they looked forward. All my gentile colleagues had a home, a family, a country, to return to. I had nothing: no parents, no family that I was aware of, no home, no town and no country. Where would I go? In our town, Jews and gentiles alike had been brutally killed. The town no longer existed. When I returned from the depths of the forests and the swamps, there were no bouquets waiting for me, not a drop of love or a glance of good will from the neighbours, no devoted parents to embrace me. For me the day of victory was a day of reckoning. Never in my life had I felt so lonely, so sad; never had I felt such yearning for the parents, family and friends whom I would never see again. I felt a deep sorrow for all my people mercilessly murdered.

I walked along the streets of Pinsk by myself, occupied with my thoughts, my mind racing with decisions to make. Elsewhere the war was far from over. After the liberation of our area, most of the Jewish partisans were enlisting in the Soviet army to continue the fight in Italy, France and the Mediterranean. For many, the struggle and suffering were to continue. The death camps were at fever pitch. Paris was not liberated till more than a month later, at the end of August 1944. And throughout the Balkans, the Soviet advance was slow. The Soviet forces, along with Tito's partisan units in Yugoslavia, were to battle desperately throughout the fall of 1944. There were still heavy battles to fight on the road to Berlin, battles wherein one could still lose one's life.

To postpone my need to think about the future, I thought I too would join the battle. I had heard that the Soviet army was dispatching "descendeurs" to be parachuted into Yugoslavia, where Nazi soldiers and Tito's partisans were still locked in mortal combat. Here the partisan movement was still active. Registration remained open for volunteers to be parachuted. I decided to register; I couldn't rest.

The day after liberation, as I walked the three kilometres to the army registration office headquarters, I met a middle-aged officer from the Soviet army. He stopped me and started a conversation. Speaking with a Soviet officer passing by was something I was used to from my years as a partisan. Who was I? Where was I from and where was I going? We talked for a long time. Though it occurred to me that he looked Jewish, he never admitted this and I never asked. But I assumed he became interested in me and my future because he recognized that I was a Jewish girl. Finally, he said, "Listen to me. You are a young girl and I know that you are alone and have nobody to help you make your decisions. You are a partisan and have already done enough fighting. Be grateful that you are alive and survived. You are a photographer. This is one of the best professions in the Soviet Union. You have an excellent future. Don't go parachuting into Yugoslavia! I am much older than you and I am giving you good advice. We might never meet again, but if you listen to me you will never forget me."

I thought for a while. Maybe this stranger was right; his advice made sense to me. I changed my mind and decided not to register to be parachuted into Yugoslavia. I decided to turn back to life without knowing what I wanted of the future.

❦

I found myself in Pinsk, a real town, again. I was overcome with a sense of unreality. Here I was, after two years of living in the forest, and I was finding that the world outside the forest was still running as though life were normal. Once the area had been liberated, the Soviet government had set about restoring the social order. People were in the streets. Business was going on as usual. Children were playing. Everything was as if the war had never even occurred, even though millions of people had been killed, including my family. I had a terrible gut-wrenching feeling at the pit of my stomach.

Former partisan leaders appointed by Soviet authorities to executive positions organized local governments in the newly liberated towns and cities. The main office in Pinsk, headed by our old partisan commander Alexei Yefimovich Kleschov, had already prepared a list of partisan leaders designated to take over the administration in the recaptured towns. I was appointed to an official government position as a photographer for the main daily newspaper of White Russia, *Bialoruskaja Pravda*, in Pinsk.

Pinsk lay just within pre-war Polish territory. Before the war, the city had had close to forty-five thousand Jewish inhabitants; now there was scarcely a Jewish soul from the pre-war population. The city of Pinsk was *Judenrein*, cleared of Jews. The windows from which my relatives and my Jewish friends had used to greet me now displayed the angry looks of strangers. Gentiles had moved into these formerly Jewish homes; they were afraid the original owners might return to reclaim them. Many houses still bore mezuzahs on their doorways, but none contained Jewish families. Wherever I turned, I felt bereavement and loss. From the streets lined with Jewish homes came the silent cry of our brothers and sisters — an imagined cry which rang incessantly in my ears.

I passed by a school at recess time. Children were running, playing, laughing and jumping — but there were no Jewish children among them. I recalled my sister's two children, buried alive by the Nazis. The whole terrible past appeared before my eyes. I rushed by quickly, wanting to get as far from the schoolyard as I could.

I went to the Soviet authorities' housing department, a newly formed office that supplied rooms and houses to people in government positions, to ask for a room. Because of my position as photographer, I would have been allowed to ask for an entire house for myself. But after my years in the woods, a single room was sufficient. I walked into the house to claim the room the housing department had assigned to me. It was in a house that before the war had been a Jewish home; I could see the mezuzah on the door frame. Evidence of the former occupants was everywhere. The silver Sabbath candlesticks were still on the buffet in the dining room. The landlord now was a gentile, of course. He was wearing a black *surdut*, the suit which chasidim wear on the Sabbath. I was shocked. Not only had all Jewish homes been appropriated, but the new inhabitants had the audacity to wear the former owners' clothes.

The woman of the house greeted me with a cold suspicious look. There was no kindly expression on her face nor warm smile — no friendliness or compassion. She obviously hadn't expected a Jewish girl to return alive into this Jewish house that she now occupied. I asked her to show me the room. She took me into a tiny room with a single bed and a small table. I told her emphatically that I would take it. I had no belongings, only the clothes on my back. There would be no suitcases, no furniture to move in, nothing but my camera — from which I was never parted.

A couple of hours later I came back to the house to find the woman standing in the doorway. In an ingenuous voice she told me that two girls, Navy officers, had taken my room. I was stunned and very angry; the room had already been rented to me.

I didn't say a word, but I was determined to show this woman that though the war went on, the Nazi rule in Pinsk was over. Anti-Semitism was no longer acceptable. I immediately went to the Admiral of the Navy. I walked in with my partisan medal pinned on and saluted. I explained to the Admiral that two of his officers had taken the room given to me by the housing department. He politely apologized; I was assured that he personally would look after the problem.

When I got back to the house, my room was vacant again. The gentile landlady of this Jewish house had suddenly changed her attitude towards me. Now she looked at me with apparent respect; she even tried to be chummy. Offers of help were extended, which I, of course, rejected. I was full of anger.

As a photo-correspondent for the *Bialoruskaja Pravda*, I was very successful. Despite the post-liberation living conditions, and despite the heartbreak and loneliness of being a Jewish survivor, my aspirations and determination had been rekindled. I felt proud of my wartime achievements and strengthened by my partisan experiences.

But before long, I became aware of the difficulties of living under a communist regime. I discovered I was the only photographer in the whole province of Pinsk. Where were the others, I wondered. The answer was that they had all been accused of being spies and had been sent to Siberia. I had already experienced this type of paranoia when I had lived in Lenin during the 1939 to 1941 Soviet occupation. I was concerned about my own welfare in this unsettling time.

In the meantime, I was being treated like a VIP everywhere I went. Towns and villages on my itinerary displayed huge posters announcing the day on which the newspaper photographer would be arriving. I took pictures of all the *stachanovices*, the award-winning workers. Portraits of the farm hands and factory workers who had done "more work in less time" were published in the newspaper. It was I who took their photos. I also took pictures for the newspaper of all of the executives, communists, party officials, and KGB officers.

When I would arrive in a village, the government authorities would hold parties in my honour. Doors were open for me everywhere I went. The first secretary of the local

Communist Party and head of the Pinsk province, Alexei Yefimovich Kleschov, my former partisan brigade commander, was not accessible to the public. For me, however, the door was always open. Kleschov considered me his friend since I had been a member of his brigade. We had struggled together and come to know each other very well. In Pinsk, I now could take advantage of this connection. I was permitted to eat in the same restaurant with Kleschov and with all of the communist officials.

Soon I became aware of the difficulties created by my lack of membership in the Communist Party. Many times I would be asked why I hadn't joined the *Komsomol*, the communist youth organization. My answer was always, "How would it look if I joined the *Komsomol*? I have a responsible adult position. The *Komsomol* is for children. In another year I will be old enough to join the regular Communist Party."

The truth was, I wasn't a communist. I also knew that if I did join the party for the sake of convenience, I would have difficulty leaving the Soviet Union when the war ended. At that point, I had aspirations of immigrating to Palestine.

⚘

By mid-summer 1944 I had found a place to stay and a steady job. My next task was to find my brother, Kopel. I knew that an ultra-observant Jew would find it difficult to survive in the uncertain atmosphere of post-liberation. I now had enough food and money to support my brother.

I decided to search the villages close to Kopel's former partisan base. Kleschov gave me the written permission I needed to travel, but there were still obstacles. My destination was about a hundred kilometres east of Pinsk where there was no regular transportation for civilians. To take a horse and wagon was dangerous; though much had been done in the larger centres to restore order, the woods were still filled with marauding bands. People were killed daily on the roads; I no longer owned a rifle.

The only way to travel was on the trains, but because of the continuing war effort only Soviet military personnel were allowed on the trains. The general public was prohibited from using the trains. Disregarding these regulations, I went to the train station and found out in which direction the trains were heading — also a military secret — and jumped on an eastbound car. The train was crammed with Soviet soldiers. Showing them my medal, I told them I had been with the Soviet partisans and was looking for my brother, who had also been with the partisans. The soldiers let me stay, treating me as one of their own, and hiding me whenever the control officers came to check for civilian passengers.

After a couple of days, my train stopped at one of the villages to change direction. I had to find another train going east. This time, I found myself among a group of nurses. I told them that I had been a nurse among the partisans. They too welcomed me and shared their food. Wherever I went the word "partisan" and my medal brought me respect and admiration.

Reaching the village where my brother Kopel's unit had been liberated took me almost two weeks. Fortunately, I arrived safely. My relief was soon to turn to disappointment. I found out that only two days earlier my brother Kopel had enlisted in the Soviet army. He had been sent to the front line. I had missed him by no more than a couple of days. Depressed and alone again, I had no choice but to return to Pinsk on another military train.

Chapter Fifteen

REUNIONS AND NEW BEGINNINGS

*B*Y THE LATE FALL of 1944 I was short of photo supplies, which were crucial to my work. Because such supplies were not available in Pinsk at the time, I had to go further afield to the larger city of Minsk more than two hundred kilometres north and east of Pinsk.

I had another reason for my interest in going to Minsk. I believed my older brother, Moishe, might be living there. I had heard rumours that there was a photographer who had been a partisan in the Minsk area. If he were still alive, I was sure I could find him. As a photographer, he would be easy to track down. He, too, would be working for the post-liberation Soviet authorities.

Again I asked Kleschov for a travel permit. Train transportation between the major centres of Pinsk and Minsk was more accessible. I didn't worry about accommodations. It was a short time after liberation and the memory of the conditions under which I had lived during the partisan years was still fresh. When and where to sleep was not a problem to me. A floor, grass, dirt — anything would be fine.

My first stop was at the government headquarters of Minsk. I wanted to find out if there was a photographer registered as working in the city. I introduced myself to one of the government representatives; he was soon able to give me the address of the official photographer. I remember feeling that luck was with me.

I went straight to the address that the official had given. It was an enormous two-storey house. The first floor looked totally abandoned, the rooms empty and cold. I went to the second floor and opened the door carefully in a typical partisan manner — without knocking. It was a large room with almost no furniture except for a big wooden table in the middle. And there he was, my brother Moishe. He was standing over the table, sorting out photographs. He looked at me with astonishment, as though I had arrived from another world.

I thanked God that my brother was still alive. We had not seen each other since spring 1942 when he had been taken by the Nazis to the Gancevich forced labour camp. We had had no contact with each other throughout our time among the partisans. Though I had tried to find him, I had never found out where he was. I hadn't even known if he were still alive. Now, late in 1944, there he stood before my eyes!

Moishe wanted to know if I knew of any other survivors from Lenin. Unfortunately, I knew of none. Most had been murdered by the Nazis, the rest later killed in the partisans. I asked if he knew of any survivors from our town. He said, "Yes, there is one young man. He lives here with me. He was also with the partisans, in command of a brigade — Morris Schulman. He works as a chartered accountant in a big government factory and lives here with me." When I heard this, my happiness doubled! I had known Morris before the war in Lenin and had always liked him. We had met once briefly in my time among the partisans.

❦

Morris (far left) with his partisan unit.

I had known Morris since the very beginning of the war and he knew my entire family. Morris had been a refugee from western Poland; he had come from Warsaw. In 1939, when the Nazis swept in through the west of Poland and occupied Warsaw, Morris had managed to escape. Among thousands of other refugees, he had made his way to Lenin which was then still safe for Jews as part of Soviet-occupied Poland.

In Lenin, Morris had worked as an accountant for a big government company. I used to see him often. Our town was small and everyone knew everyone else. He would stand on the sidewalk near his place of work, talking to friends, as I passed by during the course of my own work as a photographer. Very often when I passed him, our eyes would meet. These looks were intense, but we never spoke much.

In 1942, after the Nazis had occupied our town, Morris

was taken to the Gancevich slave labour camp, along with my two brothers Moishe and Kopel, and all the other young men of Lenin. Morris too later escaped and joined the partisans. He first joined as an underground fighter, later advancing and becoming commander of his brigade. He was very brave and his military training was excellent. Before the war, he had been an officer in the Polish army. Morris specialized in blowing up enemy trains. When westbound trains filled with livestock were blown up, Morris would return the confiscated cattle to their owners. In this way he gained many friends amongst the peasants of the area.

The fact that Morris was Jewish made his leadership difficult for many Russian partisans to accept. His position and his life were always at risk. Yet he conducted himself with great dignity and courage. When gentile partisans wanted to compliment him, they would often say that he fought like a Pole. His answer was consistent: "I am not Polish; I am a Jew and a Jew can also fight."

Morris was committed to helping the Jewish families that were hiding in the woods, bringing them food, clothing and other necessities for survival. Once he was even able to find some honey left behind by retreating Nazis which he gave to the children. Morris' commissar was prepared to kill him when he found out that Morris had given away the honey to the Jews. Seeing that he was in serious trouble, Morris fled deeper into the woods. There he was able to shoot a duck in flight. The duck was brought to the commissar, who accepted it as a peace offering. Such was life among the partisans.

We had met only once during my two years among the partisans. Travelling eastward from our base, our group of twelve, tired and hungry, had approached the village of Navozielnich. We had decided to take a chance and enter a house in the village, hoping no enemy was present. The villages in this area were safer than those around our own base. Partisans were stationed in the villages of this area and were even able to sleep in the local houses, something which we were rarely able to do in our area.

It was past midnight. All the houses were dark except for one house where light shone through the small windows. We stepped inside; the interior was one big room divided into two parts. Straw and a few blankets covered the floor of the sleeping area. The other half of the room had a glowing fire in the brick stove and a big wooden table with a bench on each side. Three partisan officers sat at the table with a map. They were deep in discussion.

We announced ourselves as we walked in. As I came closer to the table, I recognized Morris. The room was barely lit, but I knew him immediately. I smiled. Recognizing me right away, he quickly got up from the bench and gave me a warm hug. Then he introduced me to his fellow partisans.

In this strange house in the forest, our eyes met again. They reflected the horror and sadness we had each experienced in the interim. We had so much to talk about, but we said little. Morris ordered the farmer to feed us. The farmer's wife brought bread, yogurt and pickles. When Morris said, "Bring us something better," she added sour cream. We ate; we even had a drink of vodka.

Morris noticed that my feet were bound in rags. He said, "You can't walk like this. I have to get you a pair of boots." I said, "No! I don't want boots. It is much safer for me without boots." Being a partisan, he understood the danger of being killed for one's boots while separated from the larger partisan group.

We had had but little time to talk when suddenly the alarm was sounded. We heard shooting outside: we were being ambushed by Nazis. We all ran from the house. Morris' group of forty appeared from neighbouring houses; they ran in the direction of the enemy. I with my group ran in the other direction to rejoin our unit.

This is how Morris and I met for the first and only time during the partisan years. I didn't know whether he would survive nor did he know whether I would survive. As we parted, I wondered if we would ever meet again.

~

I was so happy to hear that Morris was still alive and living in Minsk with my brother; my excitement knew no bounds. Impatiently, I asked my brother where Morris was. As we were talking I heard the door open. Morris saw me right away. For a while, he remained standing in the doorway, overcome with joy. Finally he rushed over and shook hands with me. His simple handshake contained so much emotion, so much friendliness and affection. He didn't say much, but I knew that our feelings were mutual. This time the feeling was even stronger than before: it was love. Neither of us expressed it, but it was there. In that instant, Morris and I both knew that our relationship was meant to be.

Life was very intense for the recently liberated Jewish survivors. Left with little or no family, we felt a strong desire to rebuild our lives with those who were still alive. After all we had been through, there was a great immediacy in our lives — a need to repair and begin afresh. We felt an urgency to proceed quickly with whatever love was left in us.

I stayed in Minsk for a few more days, gathering my photo supplies. Morris took me out to a restaurant every day. Because of the war rationing that continued, one could not go into a restaurant to eat without special meal tickets. Since Morris had been appointed as an accountant for a large military factory, a high position, he was always able to get meal tickets.

During those few days in Minsk, I deliberated on why Morris did not talk of love or marriage. In my vulnerability, I wondered how I could be foolish enough to expect him to want to marry me. He had been a commander of a brigade, a partisan hero with many medals. He was ten years older, mature, a man. And who was I? Just a young girl. I had noticed many girls approaching him, doctors, engineers, who were so much better educated than I. Why should he propose marriage to me?

True, I was popular in Pinsk and had already had several suitors who had proposed. But I was not in love with any of them. One was a commander of a detachment; we knew each other from the partisans. This commander was a very strict military man; I was afraid of him. One day he ordered me to come to the marriage bureau with him. I was scared, too scared to say no. As we began walking to the marriage bureau, I suddenly panicked and ran away. It was a stupid way to handle the situation, but I was afraid that I would come to my senses too late. That was the last I saw of the commander.

Another suitor of mine was the mayor of Pinsk. He was a simple, good Jewish man, but an ardent communist. This was not for me. On Jewish holidays, he would not enter the synagogue but would stand outside until services were over. There was also a Jewish movie producer who flew around in a government airplane. He also proposed, asking me to come to Moscow with him to live. I declined.

I was in love with Morris. I had known him before the war; he had known my family. This meant a great deal to me. We had gone through similar experiences among the partisans. Morris also was interested in leaving the Soviet Union when the war ended and going to Palestine some time in the future.

Later, Morris told me what he was thinking at that time; why he did not propose marriage to me right away. "How could I have said I loved you? You were so young, so beautiful, so popular. I was afraid you would reject me. Why would you marry an older man, when you had your pick of so many younger men in high positions? I was afraid to ask you to marry me."

I went back to Pinsk to find a lot of work waiting for me. I was obliged to travel to several towns and villages to take pictures right away. Not quite two weeks passed when Morris came to visit me in Pinsk. He could not rest; he was afraid that he would lose me. This time, he did not wait before proposing. I was filled with happiness. We returned to Minsk and were married in my brother's house on December 12, 1944. It was difficult to find the ten Jewish men in Minsk — previously a city of many Jews — to make up the *minyan*, the quorum required for the religious wedding ceremony we wanted.

The day after the ceremony, we had to take leave of each other. I had to go back to my work in Pinsk; Morris had to remain in Minsk until he received permission to leave his position or got a company transfer to Pinsk.

Back in Pinsk, I waited anxiously but heard nothing from Morris — not a telegram or a letter, not a phone call. I began to wonder about the speed with which we got married. Maybe it was all a joke; maybe Morris didn't really care for me. I worried that he would never come back to me.

A month went by. I was walking with my camera down the street when a Soviet officer stopped me. He told me that my husband was looking for me. I could not believe it. Was it possible Morris was here in Pinsk? I went home as soon as I could. And there was Morris. He asked me what had happened, why I wasn't waiting for him at the train station. I said

Faye and Morris shortly after their marriage.

that I didn't know that he was coming. He had sent me a telegram a month ago and also had written me a letter saying that he would be coming today. The telegram came a week after his arrival, five weeks in transit. And I never received the letter.

My little room was too small for the both of us. We were able to transfer to a lovely house, a well-furnished place complete with wall hangings, carpets and beautiful tablecloths. Our life was a complete contrast to our previous hardship. We both had very good jobs, highly regarded positions. Morris, as a former high-ranking officer with the partisans, had again found a job as an accountant for a government industry. My photography was in demand; I worked very hard. We both had more than we needed in money and food.

Once after a long day at work, I returned to our house. When I opened the door, I saw a stranger lying on our kitchen floor. "Who's that?" I asked Morris. He answered that she was a Jewish woman he had come across on the street. On the way home from work, he had seen this woman lying on the sidewalk. He had stopped and asked her what was wrong. She had looked very ill; could hardly speak. She lay curled up, her face yellow. In a weak voice she had told him that she had come to Pinsk with a Russian family from the far east of the Soviet Union. She had taken care of their children, but when she became ill, they threw her out on the street. Now she couldn't walk and had no place to go. Morris had had to carry her on his back for more than a kilometre to bring her to our home. Now he asked me to see what I could do for her. We had to try to get her well.

I immediately called a friend who was a doctor. The woman had malaria. The doctor made out a prescription for her; I washed her and put her to bed. I took care of her until she recovered. She wasn't as old as she looked when she was ill, perhaps fifty at the most. It took a long time, but she got well. When she was well enough to work, she stayed with us and became our housekeeper. Sarah became part of our household. She had her own room in our house. She had grown healthy and stronger and was very happy with us, thankful to us for saving her life.

Sarah would go to the black market to buy what we needed. Times had changed so much for Morris and me. I always gave Sarah a handful of money, never counting how much. I had so much money I didn't know what to do with it; I could put nothing in the bank because I would be considered a capitalist. During our partisan years, when money had not existed for us, we managed to live without it. Now money was not the most important thing for us either.

When I took pictures of people privately, they paid me in rubles and so my pockets were always full. I could not carry a purse because my hands were occupied holding the camera and the negatives. So I had made a hole in my coat pockets and the money went down into the lining of my coat. When I came home I would reach for a handful of rubles which I would give to Sarah to buy chickens in the black market.

Morris and I invited a group of Jewish survivors to dine with us, seven or eight former partisans — we could not find any more Jewish people in Pinsk at the time. Each evening, Sarah and I served them supper. We sat around the dinner table and reminisced about our past before the war and about the hardships and atrocities we had later endured. It was a gathering of those who had suffered inhuman losses, who fought hard to survive the Nazi hell. This was the beginning of our new community, our new way of life.

⚬

I had heard nothing from my brother Kopel. All I knew was that after liberation, he had enlisted in the Soviet army, which was headed for the front line near Berlin. One day, I finally received a postcard from him. It was miraculous that this postcard reached me, since it carried only my name and no specified address. The reason that the postcard did manage to reach me was that everyone in the Pinsk area knew who I was. Kopel wrote that he had been wounded and was in a Soviet military hospital 1,400 kilometres east of Moscow: "The Nazis did not have enough explosives to kill me. All they managed to do was to tear off my toe."

Kopel had been part of a heavy artillery attack on the Nazis in January 1945. As his battalion had passed by the emptied trenches of the retreating Nazis, a small explosive had gone off under his foot, completely pulverizing the front of his boot and leaving his big toe badly wounded. With no medication or medical personnel available, he had managed to dress and bandage his own wound. Eventually Kopel was put on a military hospital train full of wounded soldiers. The train was headed for a large military hospital in the town of Opah, over 1,600 kilometres from where he had been wounded. He had been on this train for three months, travelling into the heartland of the Soviet Union. He had received no medical care on his journey. When he finally arrived at the hospital, the surgeon wanted to amputate the toe. My brother refused the amputation. The surgeon, respecting Kopel's wishes, operated on his toe instead. There was no anaesthesia available. Fortunately, the toe began to heal well with no further medical intervention. Recuperating from his trauma, Kopel wrote to me from his hospital bed in Opah.

Though I worried about Kopel's injury, I was very happy to hear that he was alive and safely away from the battles of the front line. I wanted to bring him to Pinsk where I could look after him, where I had plenty of resources and food. With my connections, I would have no problem getting him a good government job.

With the help of my brother Moishe, I managed to bring Kopel to Pinsk. But in order to remain in Pinsk indefinitely, Kopel needed a special certificate stating that he had been released from the army. The fighting continued and Kopel was still a solider in the Soviet army expected to return to active duty as soon as he was well enough. The rumour was that Soviet soldiers were now being sent to the far east of the Soviet Union to fight Japan.

I went to military headquarters where I told them that my brother was wounded and requested an official discharge.

The family: Kopel, Morris, Faye and Moishe.

They replied that he must come for a medical check-up the next day, after which they would decide if his condition warranted a discharge. If his wound had healed, he would have to go back to the army. I was worried; I knew that his toe was almost healed. If Kopel went for the military check-up, they would send him back to the army. I didn't want my brother back at the front line. I felt that he had suffered enough. There was only one thing for me to do: I had to arrange for him to leave the Soviet Union for Poland, where he would no longer be under Soviet army jurisdiction. It had to be done immediately; tomorrow might be too late.

To leave the country he would need a permit; getting a permit in the Soviet Union was not an easy thing. It was noon. I wanted to get Kopel out of Pinsk by the end of the day, so we had only a few hours left. I approached Kleschov directly, in his office: "My brother is here in Pinsk and is wounded. I need a permit for him to leave for Poland."

Kleschov was quiet for a moment. Then he asked me, "Why do you want him to go to Poland? Since he is your brother, I will give him a good government position here in Pinsk." I was on the spot and didn't know what to say. I couldn't tell him that tomorrow Kopel had to report to military headquarters and that I didn't want him back on the front line again.

Without thinking, my lips started to move: "A few days ago, my brother's wife was with a group of Soviet soldiers who left for Poland by train. She is a nurse. If he could catch the next train leaving for Poland, he might be able to catch up with her, and she would be able to look after him." My brother wasn't even married, but this was the only thing I could think of to say. Kleschov asked his secretary to make out a permit to leave the Soviet Union. I took the permit and rushed home.

Kopel had been happy at the idea of leaving Pinsk, the sooner the better. Seeing Pinsk in its present devastation was heartbreaking for him. This was the city where he had lived and studied amongst a multitude of Jews for years. In Pinsk, he felt depressed and estranged.

When I came home there was an immediate problem.

Kopel was locked out. Sarah had gone to the black market, locking the door and taking the only key with her. Neither of us could get inside. I wanted to make a parcel with some food and clothes for Kopel for his long journey to Poland. Kopel also had a sack of religious books inside; he didn't want to leave without them.

There was no time to wait for Sarah. I went into the courtyard where I had noticed a second floor window that had been left open. Next to the window stood a big old chestnut tree with many dead branches. Without hesitating, I climbed the tree and went through the open window into the house. After my experiences among the partisans, I was extremely agile at climbing. There was just one thing I had forgotten: I had just recently found out that I was pregnant.

By the time I'd climbed in the window Morris had come home. Very quickly, I made the parcel, Morris took the sack of books and all three of us went to the train station, three kilometres away. When we arrived, Kopel had just enough time to say goodbye as he limped into a train car. We had made it just in time. The train started to move and Kopel was gone.

❧

On April 30, 1945, Soviet forces entered Berlin, the capital city of Germany. Nine days later, on May 9, 1945, at one minute past midnight, all hostilities in Europe officially came to an end. The war in Europe was finally over. For me, the war had ended when I had been liberated almost a year earlier, in July 1994.

My professional life was still going well. People from the KGB came to my house to visit or to have their photos taken. My studio was located in one of the rooms of my house. I had every material thing that I could possible want. I worked hard; I needed to be busy. I didn't want the time to remember the horrible past, to walk by the dark empty houses with mezuzahs on their doors.

I was haunted by my past. Everything brought back memories of my life before the war. During the war, there had been times when I had only the clothing on my back. Now I even had four fur coats. But how could I forget that the first fur coat the Nazis had taken away from the Jews in Lenin was my sister Sonia's? Now I had more than enough food: cheese, fruit, raisins, butter and eggs. Every Soviet soldier who came to have his portrait done brought me food as a gift. But the more I had, the more painful it was for me. Where had all this food been when we had needed it in the ghetto, when my family and everyone else were starving? How could I enjoy food now?

I remembered my sister Esther's husband, the doctor, was once paid by a farmer's wife for a visit with a single egg. When he had asked her what her medical problem was, she had answered contemptuously, "You're the doctor; you should know." He had felt humiliated. Speechless, he gave her a full check-up from top to bottom, finally finding that she had a sore toe. If he had encountered such rudeness before the war, he would have thrown her out. But he had to keep quiet, because he was vulnerable as a Jew.

My brother-in-law had brought the egg home to give to my mother, who had cooked it and then carefully divided it in half, one half for each of my sister's two children. The children ate each morsel with great relish. An egg was such a delicacy in those times! The whole family stood around the children watching. We were all so hungry; we had nothing to eat, but we were happy that the children were enjoying themselves so much. Now, I had so many eggs, so much food, and nobody left alive to share it with.

Most of the people that I knew and loved were dead. In my mind and heart, however, they lived forever. Past experiences were constantly on my mind. These I could discuss with Morris. We both felt as though we were living in a cemetery. The warm glow of security in which I used to be surrounded was put out forever. We thought that perhaps, if we were to immigrate to Palestine and start a new life amongst other Jews, we could find a way to rebuild our lives.

Our prosperity, our success, our money, the house, the food — none of this made us happy. We decided to leave it all, to leave Pinsk, leave the Soviet Union. Since Morris had originally come from Warsaw, he wanted first to go there, hoping to find someone alive from his nearly two hundred family members, including parents, brothers, sisters, uncles, aunts and cousins. Surely someone must still be alive.

To leave the Soviet Union legally we had to register. When we applied to emigrate, Kleschov called and asked why I was leaving. Had we been treated poorly? Did we have some kind of resentment against the Soviet government? Had we been offended in any way?

I said that I had been treated very well, and I was not offended. I had nothing against the Soviet government. I just felt as if I were living in a cemetery. We no longer had anybody in the Soviet Union, no relatives, no friends, no Jewish people. My husband was from Warsaw. We wanted to go there to find out if any of his family had survived. Kleschov understood our plight; he did not make any difficulties for us. Our permit was duly signed. Kleschov and I bid each other a sad farewell; we had been friends for a long time.

We wanted to leave as soon as possible. Though the museum in Minsk owed me ten thousand rubles for photographs and enlargements which had not yet been paid, I did not bother to collect the money. We left everything to

Sarah, our housekeeper — all our clothes, money, and the beautiful house with all its contents. I took only my leopard-skin coat and, of course, my camera. My husband and I, with some packs on our backs, left the Soviet Union. Once again we were leaving everything behind for new wanderings, new struggles and uncertainties. We headed back into danger again — this time with no rifle or gun — back to Poland. Anti-Semitism there was rampant after the war. Many Poles were afraid that they would be forced to return Jewish property back to its rightful owners.

We came to Lodz, 460 kilometres west of Pinsk, where the majority of Holocaust survivors had congregated after the war. I contacted my brother Kopel, who was in Lodz helping to organize a new yeshiva. His injury had healed by this time and he was healthy again.

Soon after we arrived, Morris left with Kopel for Warsaw, while I stayed in Lodz. It was safer for the two of them to travel without me. We had heard of many Jews being killed in Poland after the war; I worried about Morris' and Kopel's safety. They came back after a week. During all those years among the partisans, Morris had never given up hope that he would find at least some of his loved ones in Warsaw after the war. He had wanted to tell them about his partisan experiences, how he had saved Jewish families and children hidden in the forest. Morris returned from Warsaw disappointed, depressed and bitter. He had found not one survivor from his large family. All had been killed in the gas chambers of the extermination camps.

Now we felt even more strongly that there was only one destination for us. We wanted to go to Palestine, to our people and to our land. There was no independent country of Israel at the time; the country was still called Palestine and was under British mandate. Since the British refused to allow

Jewish survivors to enter Palestine, they looked for ways to immigrate illegally. An organization called the *Bricha* had been formed in Poland to help Jewish refugees smuggle themselves into Palestine. Shortly after Morris came back from Warsaw, we joined the *Bricha* in Lodz as volunteers.

Many of the former partisans that I had known, Jewish boys and girls who had survived to the day of liberation, had enlisted in the Soviet army. Some fell on various fronts; others survived. When the war in Europe was over, many went to Palestine illegally. There they fought again — this time for a free and independent Jewish country. Many who lost their lives were buried without names: they had no passports or other documents when they entered the country illegally.

It was especially difficult to leave those countries which had been liberated by the Soviets and were now part of the communist bloc. The relationship between the Soviet Union and the other Allies had begun to deteriorate. Refugees wishing to immigrate to any country elsewhere in the world had to reach American liberated territory first before they could get visas. Germany had been divided into two countries. East Germany was occupied by the Soviet Union; West Germany by the other Allies. In West Germany temporary camps had been set up for "displaced persons," Jewish refugees in search of a new home and a new life, which were supported by the United Nations. From these camps the refugees applied for visas to countries all over the world. Others tried to make their way illegally into Palestine. It was one of the ironies of history that Jewish survivors had to get into West Germany, part of the country that they had most feared just a few months before, in order to begin a new life.

In the fall of 1945, Morris, Kopel and I left Poland, crossing through Czechoslovakia and Austria, to get to West Germany. Travelling between countries in those days was very difficult. There were major border controls; we were searched from head to toe. We had no food and no money; everything was taken away from us during these border inspections. But worst of all, we had no valid identification since our Soviet documents were not recognized outside the communist bloc. We were displaced persons, without a country and without a passport.

On one of the trains Morris, who was very depressed about losing all his family, became infuriated by the bureaucracy involved in travelling between countries. Overwhelmed, he talked back to a Polish policeman. They were ready to shoot him. When one of the policemen left for reinforcements, I managed to hide Morris under a pile of parcels. When four Polish policemen came to search for Morris, I was sitting on top of the parcels. They didn't touch me, perhaps because they saw I was pregnant. Not finding Morris, they left to search the next car. After all the years of suffering, I was nervous and exhausted. After all we had gone through, we were now again in danger. Would there never be an end to it?

At the border of Czechoslovakia, we were again searched by Polish police who were rude and brutal. In Prague, there was no room for more refugees; the DP camps were closed. We had to cross the border into Austria. In Linz we spent a very cold night in a bombed-out roofless hotel which before the war had been grand. The next day we continued on our difficult journey across yet another border into West Germany. Finally, we arrived in Landsberg, West Germany. Morris and I intended to go to Palestine. In the meantime, we were put in a refugee camp. We remained in Landsberg as displaced persons for two years. The camp was a compound of about eighteen two-storey buildings. We lived in the "partisan block." Each family lived in one room. Though we were free to come and go as we pleased, it felt like being in a ghetto again.

During our time in Landsberg, my brother Kopel was invited to head a group of senior students and open a yeshiva with the support of the *Yaad Hatzolah* of New York. New students, Holocaust survivors, arrived in Landsberg daily. During the war many had been expelled from Vilna to labour and extermination camps. They had suffered terribly. One of Kopel's students had been in the gas chambers when a Nazi opened the door and pulled him out only seconds before the gas was released. The Nazi wanted the boy for his personal servant. Kopel and his students left Germany in 1947 for New York. He lives there still today.

Morris and I remained in Landsberg where a veteran partisan group was organized. We published a magazine called *Der Wiederstand, The Resistance.* Many of our activities were in support of the establishment of the state of Israel. Our goal was to fight again, but this time to fight for our own country, for an independent, free Israel. We organized demonstrations

Demonstration in West Germany for the
formation of the State of Israel.

and rallies in support of our cause. From the food we received, we ate only enough to survive; the rest we traded with the Germans for ammunition which was smuggled into Palestine. After the war, some of the German soldiers had come home still in possession of their firearms, which they didn't need any more.

I remember we sat for days in the basement of the partisan block building, polishing and cleaning off the rust from each part of each gun and rifle. We took them apart and put them together again, making sure that they would be in good working order. It was a very familiar activity for us partisans. Each rifle or gun was vital for the fighters in Palestine. We felt that every rifle we smuggled might bring us closer to our goal of an independent Israel.

Meanwhile our own personal situation had changed. On January 27, 1946, our daughter Susan was born. The British were still unwilling to allow Jews to enter Palestine. Trying to smuggle ourselves into Palestine with a newborn baby in arms was too great a risk for us to contemplate. We had lost so many loved ones already. We were no longer prepared to join the groups that left illegally for Palestine. We had a baby now; we had new responsibilities.

EPILOGUE

*I*N EUROPE, the political conditions worsened. Tensions between the Soviet Union and the western countries heightened. Also, the Germans were not satisfied with the division between East and West Germany. In 1946 and 1947 rumours of another war abounded. After what we had already gone through, after all those horrible experiences, we did not want to get caught in another war if it were to occur, especially in Germany. We registered to immigrate to various countries around the world — anywhere in order to leave Germany. We were among the few lucky ones that Canada accepted first. We arrived in Halifax in June 1948, and from there we continued on to Toronto.

In the beginning, our new life in Canada was difficult for us. We were poor and it was hard to find work because we did not speak English. But we were young and healthy and determined to start a new life in this peaceful country, far from the troubled world we had experienced. Morris could not find work in his area of expertise. He had no documentation of his professional qualifications as a chartered accountant. Instead he worked as a labourer, carrying bricks, until he damaged a muscle in his arm. Meanwhile I was hired as a sewing machine operator at a factory which made dress shields and shoulder pads. Eventually Morris joined me in the factory as a cutter. Together we worked very hard, saving whatever we could until we were able to buy our own business, a hardware store. By then our son Sidney had been born. We ran our store for fifteen years. Finally Morris was able to get more appropriate work as a business broker.

My husband Morris, may he rest in peace, passed away in 1993. We had been married for forty-seven years. Together we lived through good times and bad times. I am now an old woman. I love my two children and my six grandchildren dearly. But my past life as a partisan, the Holocaust, the torture of our people: these I will never forget. Sometimes this bygone world feels almost more real to me than the present. I am proud of my past and of those who, like myself, were able to stand up to the enemy. That there were uprisings and resistance at all, that twenty thousand or more East European Jews fought as partisans, represented a pinnacle of bravery in the history of the Jewish people — this should never be forgotten.

And should never happen again.

❧

Faye and Morris with Susan and Sidney.

*Above: Faye with her daughter-
in-law and grandchildren.*

*Right: Faye's daughter Susan's
children.*

*Faye reunited with Jean, a former fellow
partisan; California, 1990.*

Faye Schulman with medals.

Acknowledgments of Faye's participation in the Molotava Brigade.

БССР
ПИНСКОЕ ОБЩЕСТВО
ПАРТИЗАН-ВЕТЕРАНОВ

УДОСТОВЕРЕНИЕ Серия ПН №_____

Шульман Фаина

М. П.

Владелец удостоверения являлся партизаном Отечественной войны 1941—1945 гг., действовавшим в глубоком тылу врага в отряде _____ *им. Молотова* _____ бригады, входящих в состав Пинского партизанского соединения, командиром которого был Герой Советского Союза генерал-майор Корж Василий Захарович.

Председатель Пинского
общества партизан Д. Удовиков
ветеранов
Секретарь общества Е. Пчелка

Для Пинского общества партизан служит официальным документом.
Остается в семье партизана на вечное хранение.

НАШИМ БОЕВЫМ ПОДРУГАМ ПАРТИЗАНКАМ
Шульман Фаина

Мы, партизаны мужчины, рады поздравить Вас, наших дорогих, замечательных, отважных «девчат» с днем 8 Марта. Не все из Вас ходили в бой с винтовкой. И не потому что боялись. Нет Вы не боялись. Но командование не хотело Вами рисковать, хотя каждая из Вас умела обращаться «со стрельбой». Вы были нам нужны для создания послебоевого партизанского уюта у костра... Мы понимали что Вам было трудней, чем мужчинам на фронте. Ибо ничего готового у Вас не было: ни обмундирования, ни медикаментов, ни кухонных принадлежностей. Ни у каждой даже было личное оружие — пистолет. На всё нужна была фантазия, а её у Вас хватало.

Мы помним Вашу душевную красоту, и прекрасный внешний вид, который Вы пронесли через годы, через расстояния. Мы мысленно крепко Вас целуем и вместе с поцелуем передаём (тоже мысленно) букет алых роз. Вы это заслужили. Доживем до лучших времён и вручим каждой из Вас настоящие живые цветы.

Примите самые лучшие пожелания от партизан мужчин, воевавших с Вами. Здоровья Вам, неувядаемой молодости, успехов в семейных делах, благополучия в личной жизни.

До встречи летом этого года.
8 марта 1993г.

СОВЕТ ПИНСКОГО ОБЩЕСТВА
ПАРТИЗАН — ВЕТЕРАНОВ

Appreciation of women's contribution in the home, on the front and as health care workers, from the government of the USSR.

Feb. 20, 1941.

Dear Mr. Eisenberg:

This is to inform you that the necessary
arrangements about bringing Rabbi Lazebnik
are about to be completed, as your sister
from Baltimore, Mrs. Friedman, promised to
give $180.00, which pay the way from Kowno
to Japan. Another friend from New Yrok has
sent already the rest of the money, that is
to pay the way from Japan to America.

With the hope to see Rabbi Lazebnik here
soon, we remain,

sincerely yours,

*Confirmation for Faye's brother to emigrate to USA via Japan.
Shortly after this card was sent, Rabbi Lazebnik was killed.*

Ветерану
Великой Отечественной войны
ДОРОГОЙ БОЕВОЙ ДРУГ!

Тов. *Шульман Фаина*

Пинское общество партизан-ветеранов
награждает Вас грамотой за активные боевые
партизанские действия в глубоком тылу врага
против немецких захватчиков во время Отечественной войны 1941—1945 гг., а также в
связи с 45-летием Победы советского народа и
46-летием освобождения любимой Белоруссии,
где прошла наша боевая молодость.

Председатель Пинского общества
партизан-ветеранов — Л. Удовиков
Секретарь Пинского общества
партизан-ветеранов — Е. Пчелка

Июля 1990 г.

*From the Russian government, honouring Faye's war activities
deep in enemy occupied territories.*

Faye telling Canadian high school students
about her partisan experiences; 1993.

OTHER BOOKS FROM SECOND STORY PRESS